# ᴄᴇ 10 Tips On ᴈᴐ
# How NOT to Talk to
# Your Kids About Sex

## AUDREY WERNER RN, B.S.N., M.A.

Foreword written by Author, and Co-Founder of Growing Kids International
### Anne Marie Ezzo

# 10 Tips on How NOT to Talk to Your Kids About Sex

Published by

RHEMA Publishing House.™
rhemapublishinghouse.com
PO Box 1244 McKinney, TX 75070

For information about special discounts available for
bulk purchases, sales promotions, and educational needs, contact
Audrey Werner, PO Box 1244, McKinney, Texas 75070.

ISBN: 978-0-9983064-4-5

eBook ISBN: 978-0-9983064-5-2

Cover and Interior Design: Lisa Thomson

# Endorsements

"Audrey Werner has written a refreshing, readable book on sexuality for churches and for parents to help them grapple with the unrelenting attack on purity they and their children face daily. It is a blessing to know it can be read without fear or shame, but Godly enlightening."

**- Dr. Judith Reisman**
Author of *Kinsey, Sex and Fraud* (1990), *"Soft" Porn Plays Hard Ball* (1991),
*Stolen Honor, Stolen Innocence* (2013), *Sexual Sabotage* (2011), *Kinsey, Crimes, &
Consequences* (2000), drjudithreisman.com
Founder of the Institute for Media Education
Director - Child Protection Institute - Liberty University School of Law

"I wish I had been able to study the information in this powerful, positive, palatable book years ago when I was raising my children. It would have reduced my husband's and my stress talking about the sensitive subject of sex. But, it's not too late for our grandchildren. Take the embarrassment and stress out of this necessary task! Read this book and see how positive it is to talk about this subject God's way."

**- Dr. Thelma Wells**
Founder of A Woman of God Ministries and
Generation Love-Divine Explosion
Speaker, Author, Professor, TV Host (NRB and TBN Television)
Former "Women of Faith" Conference Speaker

"In this book, Audrey Werner uses the words 'purity' and 'pure' more than sixty times. Her theme reflects the core Biblical standard for living the highest, wisest, most satisfying and ennobling life possible. That is the kind of life loving parents want for their children. It is the kind of life the Heavenly Father wants for His children.

Purity of body, mind and spirit are the core components of an ennobling existence. For most young people, the body gets far more attention than the mind or the spirit—it's a fact of human existence. It stands to reason that maintaining purity of the body during one's youth is mostly focused on sexuality. The outcome of that focus has the greatest impact on the development of the mind and spirit.

What you will learn about sexual purity by reading this book may very well change your entire understanding of what the Psalmist meant when he addressed youth's most critical challenge: 'How can a young man [person] keep his way pure? By keeping it according to Your word' (Psalm 119:9)."

**- Dennis D. Frey, Th.D.**
President Master's International University of Divinity

"Eunice and I appreciate your love of God and Country. Your dedication is exemplary. Your love of our children born and unborn is remarkable, and your work of educating the Church on behalf of restoring legal protections for marriage, women and children is gratifying. Thanks for all you do for the RSVP America, First Principles Press and Matthew XVIII."

**- Colonel Ronald D. Ray, USMCR (Ret.)**
Former Deputy Assistant Secretary of Defense
during the Reagan Administration

"Thank you Audrey Werner for carrying the torch forward to awaken the church which, so often, is a thankless mission. Colonel Ray always said there's a banality to evil. It is only reintroduced in a thin disguise in each generation, but it's the same old hell that's been lurking since the Garden. The RSVP America archive became the focus of our work in 2006, after actively pursuing the campaign from 1998-2003. We were directed to sort, scan and upload thousands of documents—all of the RSVP America papers and materials—to serve as 'crumbs along the path' for future generations to follow so they don't have to rediscover the fraud and crime that changed Godly American law and public policy that once protected Marriage, Women and Children. Audrey, your Matthew XVIII work continues to call attention to the good news of God's perfect plan for the Marriage institution and its protections for His most vulnerable."

**- Eunice Ray**
Founder and Director of RSVP America

"It has been said that God uses people in all stages of His work: those who plant the seed, those who water while God causes all things to grow. So it is with Audrey's book. Audrey watered faithfully year after year!

More than twenty years ago I asked Audrey to look at the *Learning About Sex* series from CPH. As a Mom, I was greatly disturbed and angered by the content of these books. Audrey was equally incensed, but the scale of influence Audrey brought to this endeavor was monumental. I love how God prepared Audrey for this mission. He wove her talents and interests in the medical field and she became a nurse. But not just any kind of nurse—a County Health nurse. He gave her all sorts of experiences that solidified her ability to speak with authority on the subject. He also enflamed her with a love of His Word—and it was weaving the two together that makes this book so monumentally important.

Christians have been deceived by the world's 'knowledge.' Audrey has replaced it with God knowledge! So much more effective and so much more rewarding for parents. May your life and the lives of your children be blessed by this book. My prayer is that after reading this book you recognize the lies of the world and take a stand for your children. Well done, Audrey, this has become your lifelong mission— saving the innocence of young souls!"

**- Patricia Raezler BA, MA**
Director of Westmaple Preschool


"We parents, today, are raising our children immersed in a culture of every kind of sexual depravity. On top of that, most of us haven't even experienced true purity, ourselves. A spirit of confusion moves powerfully, even amongst the faithful. *Ten Tips on How NOT to Talk to Your Kids about Sex* shines the light of God's Word on all of these matters, and brings them into crystal clear focus."

**- Roel and Robyn van Eck**
parents of 7 children

"I have seen the results of a generation taught sex education from a personal, spiritual, and societal view point.

*10 Tips on How NOT to Talk to Your Kids About Sex* makes objective what I have known through personal and pastoral experience. Audrey gives us a good guide for parents to both protect their children from the assaults of the devil and the world, and to teach them purity according to the Word of God. I recommend this book not only for parents, but also for church professionals and leaders, so that all of us might wake up to the dangers of sex education, even when it is cloaked in 'Christian' verbiage."

**- Pastor Mark Cutler**
Trinity Lutheran Church, Kalispell, MT

*Dedicated to my children,*

*their generation, and*

*future generations*

# Acknowledgements

First, I want to thank our Lord and Savior Jesus Christ—He uses the simple to confound the wise, the weak to defeat the strong. I pray God uses this book to take on man's view of human sexuality and destroy the lies and deceit at the foundation of the sexual revolution—specifically sex education.

I want to thank my husband Joe who has been my protector and encourager even when this ministry has been costly for the family, and my children who have been my inspiration and hope for the future.

To the many friends and colleagues who helped me throughout the process of gathering information for this book:

- Eunice Ray, founder of RSVP America, who spent countless days equipping me (and others) to take on the Kinsey legacy in the world;

- Colonel Ronald D. Ray, USMC (ret.)—Deputy Assistant Secretary of Defense during the Reagan Administration, Founder of First Principles Press, and author of such historical materials as *Endowed by Their Creator: A Collection of Historic American Military Prayers: 1774-present.* He has been an invaluable encourager to me and has been a courageous patriot for America;

- Dr. Judith Reisman and Dr. Linda Jeffrey who took time training and teaching me about the sexual revolution and how Kinsey's teaching has negatively affected our laws and culture;

- Gary and Anne-Marie Ezzo of *Growing Families International* whose courses have helped my husband and me raise children who have a heart for the Lord. They have also been wonderful supporters of my message and ministry;

- To the women who have gone before me to expose the origins and dangers of sex education: Claire Chambers, author of *The SIECUS Circle;* Randy Engel, author of *Sex Education–The Final Plague;* Karen Booth, author of *Forgetting How to Blush;* Gloria Lentz, author of *Raping of Our Children: The Sex Education*

*Scandal;* Linda Bartlett, author of *The Failure of Sex Education in the Church: Mistaken Identity, Compromised Purity;* Dr. Miriam Grossman, author of *You're Teaching My Child What?;* and Mrs. Woodallen Chapman, author of *How Shall I Tell My Child?*

I also want to thank my friends and prayer partners who have prayed for, encouraged, and supported me in this surprising journey. Your friendship has meant more than you can possibly imagine!

Lastly I want to thank Karen Lindwall Bourg of Rhema Biblical Counseling Center and Jimmy and Diana Richards for their support and encouragement in writing this book. This book would not have been possible without you!

# Contents

# Foreword

As parents and educators, it's important to understand that "sexual knowledge" is not innocent knowledge, because sexual knowledge cannot be separated from moral knowledge that regulates human emotions and responses.

Every child has the right to live in a safe world where he or she is not assaulted physically, emotionally, sexually or morally—a world where a child is not taken advantage of or over-powered and forced to accept unsolicited teaching regarding his or her sexuality.

But how do we protect children from intrusive, uninvited, inappropriate forces that can injure their emotional and moral capacities? Who determines what is inappropriate, what is good, reasonable, protective—and what crosses the line? What can and should parents be doing at home to protect and prepare their children for the moral and sexual onslaught prevalent in our current society, without robbing their children of their innocence? Or, as the current generation of parents are being told, "Leave it to the professionals and we'll provide your children comprehensive sex education classes in the comfort of their classroom."

Because of the subject matter, many parents are all too willing to abdicate their position of primary teacher and influencer of their children. They believe the lie that the "experts" have a better way, and therefore release their children to hear information that introduces them to vocabulary and concepts about their sexual identity that a previous generation couldn't have dreamed of. Nor would they have even known the meanings of half of what is being taught to today's children as "fact."

While parents in the twenty-first century are attempting to process all these changes regarding our sexuality, most are completely unaware of where this whole *sex ed* thing began. After all, it would have been during their parents' youth, starting back in 1964, that the idea of sex education was introduced into the public sector: information based on research by a Dr. Alfred Kinsey. It was his "scientific studies" that provided a new view of sexuality outside the context of marriage and children. Prior to Kinsey, writings that reflected the American notion of human sexuality were presented as, **God's Life Process** or the **Marital Act,** and everything else was known as **Carnal Knowledge.** We went from viewing man as an individual created in the image of God—with dignity and what we call biblical anthropological context—to viewing man as part of Zoology, just higher up in the animal kingdom.

So, we ask, "How can we teach our children a biblical view of sexuality, when from a very early age they are saturated with details and images that constantly challenge the very concept of biblical purity?" Before that question can be answered, parents and educators need to understand how we got here—and then what we can do about it. That is what Audrey Werner is presenting in *10 Tips on How NOT to Talk to Your Kids about Sex.*

Within the pages of this book Audrey shares not only her own journey of discovery about the foundations of the current sex education movement, but also the agenda behind it. As you read Audrey's systematic and logical progression, the evidence becomes overwhelming that America is on the wrong track when it comes to sex education. Your emotions may go between anger at being duped by the *experts,* to helplessness in thinking *but how can I make a difference and what can be done now?!* Well, if enough of us join Audrey, and others, in this battle, we *can* make a difference. Audrey herself has said "Who am I? I'm just a mom." Well, there is nothing like waking up the "Mama bear" in every Mom who finds out her precious children's innocence is being violated—all under the guise of "education."

Audrey Werner, RN, B.S.N., M.A. and MOM, decided to make a difference as one ordinary person seeking Truth. Within *10 Tips on How NOT to talk to Your Kids about Sex,* she will expose the darkness presented through Kinsey's fraudulent science that has found its way into Christian sex education materials, and then inspire you as a parent and educator to return to sharing with children about God's life process in a modest, biblical way. As a parent educator for over thirty years, I am confident this will be one of those books that will be life changing for you, your children, and yes—even your grandchildren.

**For such a time as this** are we living—and we *can* make a difference.

Anne Marie Ezzo
Author and Co-Founder of Growing Families International

# Prelude

Did the title catch you off guard? How **NOT** to Talk to Your Kids about Sex? Most speakers and authors today title their talks and books around the theme, "**How to** talk to your kids about sex." Some well-meaning Christians add to that title, "From a Biblical Perspective" or they use the term "biblical sexuality." But how much of the information they share is biblical and how much is from man's hollow, deceptive philosophy?

How do you feel about giving your child the "sex talk?" Are you uncomfortable at the thought of it—or even dreading it? Do you have memories of your parent squirming through this talk with you or did they throw a book at you and tell you to read it? Then, once you received "the talk," do you remember how you felt? Were you grossed out, disgusted, or were other emotions awakened in you?

Parents, today you are being encouraged to get over or push through any discomfort and give "the talk" because you need to make sure that your kids know about sex before someone else tells them. But do you wonder why you have this discomfort?

What if I told you leaders from Planned Parenthood (the world's largest abortion industry), the American Humanist Association, and those who support pedophilia and pornography were behind the development of sex education? Would that make you feel better about talking to your kids graphically about sex? I would hope not.

As parents, we want what is best for our children. Honest research and history have shown that the traditional family has always been the foundation of any successful nation. People who limit themselves to one partner and delay sex until marriage have no venereal diseases at all and seem to not only stay married longer but have a stronger commitment to the institution of marriage. Research and history have also proven that children thrive in homes where there is a mom and dad under one roof.

We live in crazy times. Today responsibilities have been substituted for sexual rights, and God's Word has been replaced with feelings. We live in a world with the theme "if it feels good, do it," and sexual agendas are being promoted daily in schools and through the media.

It is hard being a parent! So how do we protect our children from a world thrown into moral chaos and how do we prepare our children for the best possible outcome? Do we educate them in sex, abstinence, or purity? These are some of the important decisions parents must make.

There is hope! We have the most powerful tool available to us, and that is God's Word. That tool is more powerful than any double edged sword (Hebrews 4:12). In Ephesians 6:17, Paul refers to it as "the sword of the Spirit, which is the word of God." Yet, I believe Christians today often underestimate the power of this tool.

The problem with many Christian resources today is that oftentimes unaware, authors have attempted to mesh God's Word with words from the *experts on sex.* After years of research I have found that these "experts" had a plan to sexualize a nation they believed to be too Victorian and repressed. Looking at today's society we see that sexual immorality is rampant, even within the church. God advises His people:

> If My people who are called by My name, will humble themselves, and pray and seek My face, and **turn from their wicked ways,** then I will hear from heaven, and will forgive their sin and heal their land. - II Chronicles 7:14

In this book I hope to prove why we can no longer rely on this deadly combination which has been named "Human Sexuality from a biblical Perspective." It has been especially disastrous in the area of sex education, where vulnerable children have been exposed to materials that were intended not only to awaken love before its time (Song of Songs 2:7 and 3:5), but have taught the last few generations to replace biblical love with lust.

We are at a critical point in our nation, where Christians are now being asked to "go into the closet." We are being told to no longer adhere to God's biblical standards but to accept new and evolving morality. Religious freedom is in jeopardy, and we need the Lord now more than ever to intervene; but we have a vital part in this revival as well.

It is my prayer that this book gives you answers and true scriptural reference, void of man's philosophy, on what we are to convey to our children. It is my prayer that parents will be able to equip their children, using God's Word, to take on the devil's schemes and help their children remain pure for the person God intended them to be with. It is my prayer that young people will be immersed in seeking out God's plan for their lives and not be involved in various sexual sins.

If parents become the primary educators of their children again and teach God's standard of purity, this generation of children can restore what the cankerworm has eaten away. God's design for the family can be restored, and God's people can influence the world around them for good and not evil.

*Only be strong and very courageous, that you may observe to do according to all the law which Moses My servant commanded you; do not turn from it to the right hand or to the left that you may prosper wherever you go. - Joshua 1:7*

# Introduction

*My people are destroyed for lack of knowledge: because you
have rejected knowledge, I also will reject you from being
priest for Me: because you have forgotten the law of your
God, I also will forget your children.*
*– Hosea 4:6*

My name is Audrey Werner, and I was one of those nurses who
taught sex education in the public and parochial schools from
elementary through high school. Because my husband was a
Family Life Pastor, I also taught "Christian sex education" in Sunday
school classes. In order to teach this in this country, one has to be
certified by "experts" in sex education. I was further told during
my educational training that parents weren't doing their job, so it
was up to us to teach kids about sex in value neutral terms. The
"experts" also told me that by educating children in their sexuality,
I would help decrease the teen STD (Sexually Transmitted Disease)
and pregnancy rates.

Ironically, my next job in nursing was working in the STD/HIV/
Pregnancy Testing clinic where my eyes were opened to the result
of sex education. It was not as I had been told; as a matter of fact,
the opposite was true, as it seemed the more sex education was
given to children, the earlier and more sexually active they became.
My colleagues and I witnessed the incidence of date-rape exploding
in the mid-1990s, and by the late 1990s mandatory HIV tests were
required of ten-year-old boys, who were alleged of raping two- and
four-year-old girls!

During that season of my life, my husband was serving as a Family
Life pastor in the Lutheran Church. We had been Lutherans all
our lives and attended Lutheran schools. While in school, we were
taught a "Christian" sex education program called the *Learning
About Sex* (*LAS*) series. Even during our high school years, despite
all of this *education*, I noted that purity was not a standard that was
kept among my peers or adults. In 1997, as a result of witnessing the
*rise* of STDs and the fact that our oldest son was about to enter a

Lutheran school where the *LAS* series was taught, I was motivated to put on my research hat and began to look into the origins of sex education.

My discovery was that sex education was an integral part of a much larger plan; revolutions don't happen overnight, and the sexual revolution was no exception—it didn't *just occur* in the 1960s. The revolutionaries behind this movement spent years planning it. This revolution, which really began in the 1920s, is a fascinating topic to cover—but for the sake of time, we will mainly focus on one aspect of it, sex education, in this book.

As my investigation went deeper, I found that one man, Alfred Kinsey, was considered the father of the sexual revolution. He proclaimed that "children were sexual from birth" and thus began the legalization of teaching sex to children. Kinsey conducted sex studies in the 1930s and 1940s, and as a result, laws that once protected women, children, and the institution of marriage, were removed and replaced with this new teaching.

Dr. Judith Reisman, considered one of the top authorities on Kinsey, and staff from RSVP America (Restoring Social Virtue and Purity to America), uncovered the fact that Kinsey's "science" was actually fraudulent. For example, **he gathered data from pedophiles who raped children over a 24 hour period of time and concluded, "Children are sexual from birth."** Based on that premise, children were then taught graphically about sex.[1]

In 1964, the *Sex Information and Education Council of the United States* (SIECUS) was launched at the Kinsey Institute and became the worldwide authority on sex education. Former President of Planned Parenthood Mary Calderone was the co-founder of SIECUS, and she worked with others who were dedicated to promoting eugenics, communism, and humanism.[2] The *Playboy Foundation* provided the first of several grants to SIECUS to ensure that children were educated in sex.[3] Lester Kirkendall, former President of the

---

[1] For more information go to www.rsvpamerica.org, www.drjudithreisman.org, and you can access "Kinsey's Pedophile's," a British Documentary on You Tube.
[2] Those who believed in eugenics, communism, and humanism are listed in Claire Chambers, *The SIECUS Circle-A Humanist Revolution*, Western Islands, Belmont, MA, 1977
[3] Judith Reisman, Ph.D., *Kinsey: Crimes & Consequences*, The Institute for Media Education, Inc., 2000, pp 176-177

American Humanist Association and Kinsey disciple, once on the Board for Planned Parenthood, also led SIECUS.

The above paragraph should be disturbing for any parent, because the industries and organizations that financially benefit from children becoming sexually active at an early age actually developed the idea of sex education. Sex education was designed to titillate children and adults to explore all forms of sexuality, not to educate in hygiene or prevent diseases. In sex education classes, children were taught to consider sexual pleasure outside of marriage, get an abortion if a conception occurred, and explore every type of sexual lifestyle (LGBTQ).

Dr. Miriam Grossman, a Child and Adolescent Psychiatrist, also confirms where sex education came from, and opens her book with a dire warning: "Parents, if you believe that the goals of sexuality education are to prevent pregnancy and disease, you are being hoodwinked."[4] Given that sex education has been in existence for over 60 years, we have plenty of data which validates the results.

On the next three pages are charts showing the moral decline in America, and you can see the direct correlation between implementation of sex education through SIECUS in 1964—when we began to talk to kids about sex—and the large increase in teen pregnancy and venereal disease rates from that point on.

---

[4] Miriam Grossman, M.D., *You're Teaching My Child What?* (Washington, D.C., Regnery Publishing, Inc., 2009. p. 7

## Sexually Transmitted Diseases, Gonorrhea - Age Group 10-14

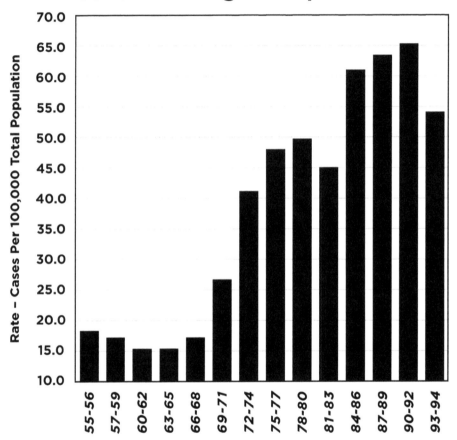

**3-Year Range**

Basic data from Statistical Abstracts of the United States, and the Department of Commerce, Census Bureau

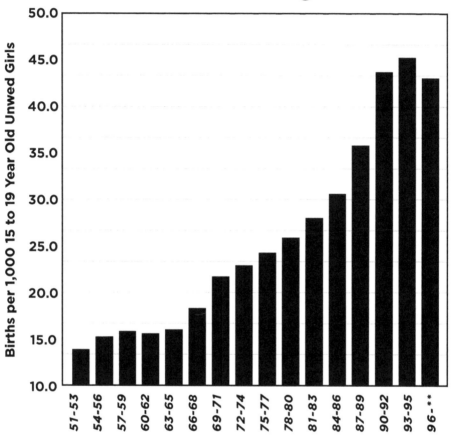

# Birth Rates for Unwed Girls
# 15-19 Years of Age

**3-Year Range**

Basic data from Statistical Abstracts of the United States, and the Department of Commerce, Census Bureau

**1996 is latest published data

# Pregnancies to Unwed Girls Under 15 Years of Age

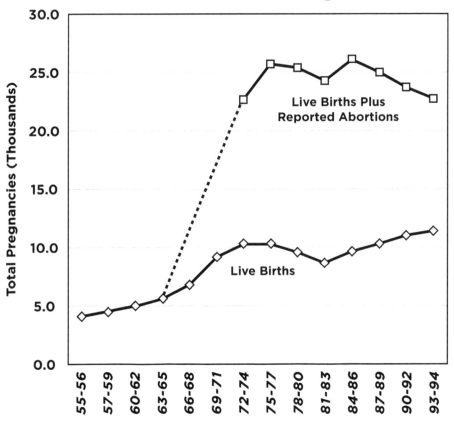

**3-Year Range**

Basic data from Statistical Abstracts of the United States, and the Department of Commerce, Census Bureau

Today, the CDC reports that we have the highest rates of recorded sexually transmitted infections ever in the history of recording such statistics.[5] It is also interesting to note here that as those who supported the sexual revolution wanted to elevate sex outside of marriage, they had to downplay the risks involved. The term "sexually transmitted *diseases*" was once used, but those who believe in sexual freedom thought this word was too harsh, so they changed it to "sexually transmitted *infections*"— because everybody gets an infection at some point—and you can simply get medications to treat infections: *right?*

A well-known Pediatric and Adolescent Physician, Dr. Meg Meeker, reports the results of treating children as if they are *sexual from birth* and even goes so far as to reveal how sexual activity outside of marriage is **killing them**. She reports:

- 1 out of every 5 adolescents is living with an STD.

- In 1960 a shot of penicillin could kill the two known STDs, syphilis and gonorrhea.

- Today there are no simple cures or no cures at all.

- The CDC considers the STD epidemic a multiple epidemic of at least 25 separate diseases (50 plus with the different strains of viruses).

- Human Papilloma Virus, HPV, just one STD, is directly responsible for 99.7% of the cervical cancer cases with nearly 5000 deaths each year.

- 80% of STD infected kids are unaware they have an STD.

- Half of all new HIV infections are infecting our youth (male and female).

- Condoms do not offer protection for most STDs.[6]

---

[5] See http://www.breitbart.com/big-government/2016/10/20/std-rates-united-states-reach-record-high/
[6] Meg Meeker, M.D., *Epidemic-How Teen Sex is Killing Our Kids*, (Washington, D.C., Regnery Publishing, Inc., 2002

I realize that I am writing to the generations who have been in those uncomfortable sex education classes or squirmed when your parent tried to give you that "sex talk." For the past fifty to sixty years we have been following the sex industry's advice, and let's be honest— how many can report that they waited until marriage or had only one partner in their lifetime?

I lament over the abortions, the venereal diseases, the infertility, the divorces, the rapes (or "sexual assaults" as we call it today because "rape" is too harsh a word), the suicide attempts that have resulted from treating children as sexual beings; it has been disastrous! It is time to return to the old ways—when children could be children, STD rates were lower, and marriages lasted "until death do we part."

Last year I was asked to make a presentation on sex education to a state representative from Texas, along with some of his staff, who was motivated to block Planned Parenthood from becoming the primary sex educator in all our schools. For an hour I went through my powerpoint presentation showing the history of sex ed, who developed it, its intent—and most importantly, how costly it has been for kids of the last few generations. At the end of the presentation, his Chief of Staff—who realized that Planned Parenthood had been in the schools since the beginning of SIECUS in 1964—asked, "You don't mean to get rid of *all* sex education in the schools?" Given what I now know about sex education, I confidently said, "Yes, I do!"

So I challenge you to be diligent; do the research and find out for yourself where the graphic direct approach to teaching children about sex came from. Search the older books that were written for parents before the sexual revolution, and research who the "experts" in sex education actually were. I guarantee you will find we have been lied to and deceived, and more importantly, lured away from the biblical principles God laid out for us in His Word.

*Test all things, hold fast what is good. Abstain from every form of evil. - I Thessalonians 5:21-25*

**Suggested Resources**

*RSVP America Training Manual,* www.rsvpamerica.org

*Kinsey, Crimes, & Consequences* and *Sexual Sabotage: How One Mad Scientist Unleashed a Plague of Corruption and Contagion on America* by Judith Reisman

*The Global Sexual Revolution: Destruction of Freedom in the Name of Freedom* by Gabriele Kuby

*You're Teaching my Child What?* by Dr. Miriam Grossman

*Forgetting How to Blush: United Methodism's Compromise with the Sexual Revolution* by Karen Booth

*Epidemic: How Teen Sex is Killing our Kids* by Dr. Meg Meeker

# Chapter 1
# Tip 1
## More is Caught than is Taught

*If the foundations be destroyed, what can the righteous do?*
*– Psalm 11:3*

In the introduction of this book, I shared the facts about sex education: who developed it and the intent behind giving sex education to children. Hopefully, that information has provided you, as a parent or educator, enough motivation to avoid using any current resources dealing with sex education and discover how we can raise pure kids using God's Word. But before looking at some Tips, there is a first step we must take—we need to take account of our own actions.

Maybe a story about what I am talking about would help bring clarity to that step. When I wanted to learn how to pray for my husband, I purchased Stormie Omartian's book *The Power of a Praying Wife*. I couldn't wait to learn how to better help and encourage my husband. However, I was quickly humbled; Stormie talked a great deal about being a godly wife **before** I could start praying for my husband. Was I aligned with God and His Word as a Christian wife, or was I ignoring my sins and only concentrating on fixing my husband? That first chapter was very enlightening for me.

The same is true for us as parents; before we can teach our children about purity, we must repent of past failures and make sure that we are modeling purity to our kids. Many of us comprise the first generation exposed to wide-scale sex education, and we live with the tragic consequences. The difficult question to answer is: How many of us are carrying around sexual sins that we have never repented of?

In the book *The Battle Plan for Prayer*, the Kendrick brothers give us something to consider:

> *Victory necessitates repentance. Repentance helps you stand strong against temptation. But there's a difference between being tempted by something and being tormented by something. Everyone is tempted. Jesus was. You will be. It's not a sin to be tempted. But if the enemy is constantly tormenting you with something, there's a good chance unconfessed sin from your past has given him a foothold (a network of lies) in your heart (II Corinthians 10:3-5). Though the truth will set us free, lies can keep us in bondage.[7]*

I believe children of this generation are under more spiritual attack than any previous generation, and the deception or techniques for leading little ones to sexual sin has been perfected by those who don't want our children to follow Christ. You and I had fornication and abortion sold to us; our children face much more. They need healthy parents to help equip them for those attacks.

Having had the opportunity to travel across the country speaking on purity, I can't tell you how many parents have told me, "I wish I had heard this purity message when I was young, because my life would have turned out differently." **Don't allow past sins to keep you silent in regards to encouraging a pure life for your children!** If you do, then Satan has accomplished his goal: he will move forward any legacy of sexual immorality that began in your family and will pass it down to the next generation.

**The time is now for us to return to God's Word and do what He asks us to do while on this earth.** I look to our Lord as a loving parent who set up boundaries for us so that we will not be hurt. Those who promoted the sexual revolution tried to convince us that abstaining from fornication was wrong and even harmful. God knew otherwise. Just as a parent knows that allowing your children to run in the street could get them killed, God knew what would happen to us if we turned from His Word.

---

[7] Stephen and Alex Kendrick, *The Battle Plan for Prayer*, B & H Publishing, Nashville, TN, 2015, 174-175

He knew if we were in multiple sexual relationships, it would be hard to remain married to only one person. He knew the pain we would experience if we went through a divorce. Actually, He is the one who designed our bodies down to every last molecule. He gave us bonding hormones which are triggered during the procreative act to seal the bond between a husband and wife: oxytocin for women and vasopressin in men.[8]

God gave us the path that we should follow:

> *For this is the will God, your sanctification: that you should abstain from sexual immorality; that each of you should know how to possess his own vessel in sanctification and honor, not in passion of lust, like the Gentiles who do not know God; that no one should take advantage of and defraud his brother in this matter, because the Lord is the avenger of all such, as we also forewarned you and testified. God did not call us to uncleanness, but in holiness. Therefore he who rejects this does not reject man, but God, who has also given us His Holy Spirit. – I Thessalonians 4:3-8*

God calls all of us to holiness, and when we are involved in sexual sin, there is *deadness* in our souls. We are pulled toward the flesh and away from the Holy Spirit (Galatians 5:17). Since the inception of the sexual revolution we have been persuaded to forget God's direction and "just do it."

Jesus commanded man to not look lustfully upon a woman—because if he did, it was as if he was committing adultery with her in his heart (Matthew 5:27). He told us this because He is the one who designed our brains, and He knew that viewing pornography could actually cause neuroplastic changes that could affect behavior and lead men to the most abhorrent of acts.[9]

Pornography is widely accepted today and easy for children to access. The "what I do behind closed doors doesn't affect anyone else" rationale that is promoted in society, and unfortunately often in the church, is a travesty! I am surrounded by Christian families

---

[8] Joe S. McIlhaney, Jr. M.D. and Freda Bush, M.D., *Hooked: New Science on How Casual Sex is Affecting Our Children*, Northfield Publishing, Chicago, 2008, 35-43
[9] Norman Doidge, M.D., *The Brain That Changes Itself*, Penguin Books, NY, NY, 2007, 103-131

that have fallen apart because of dad's or mom's involvement in pornography. It is time that we turn from these wicked ways so God can do some healing!

Now that you know where sex education came from, what it was intended to do to (more about this in later chapters), and the fact that we are the first generation to have gone through it, there are further questions we must ask ourselves:

Am I currently dabbling in sexual sin?

What is my home environment like? Is it free of sexual images or words (music, television, computer, magazines, and books)?

If you are providing your children the tools to avoid sexual sin, then you want to make sure that you are living a life of purity in front of them and providing an environment that reflects Christ—not a toxic environment that will only bring confusion to your children's minds and hearts.

One of the instructions given in an airplane by the flight attendant is that if the plane should have a sudden change in air pressure and the oxygen masks drop down, parents are to put their own oxygen masks on first and then put the mask on their child. A parent who has been incapacitated by the lack of oxygen is of no help to their child.

I liken this to what the sexual revolution has done to a generation of parents. Sexual sin has slain many people in and outside of the church. We are the first generation to have been exposed to sex education, and many of us—upon being indoctrinated with that "sexual identity"—went down dark paths we never thought we would travel, whether it be fornication, abortion, pornography or addiction. I liken God's Word to oxygen—*we are dying from the lack of God's direction; our families are falling apart and our nation is crumbling in every area.*

**It is time for our generation of parents to get healthy and put on that oxygen mask so we can help the next generation to avoid the immoral disasters that our generation has had to endure.**

In Ezekiel 37, God brings Ezekiel to a valley full of dry bones and then has him prophesy over the dry bones. The Holy Spirit fills the valley, the bones come together, the bodies are repaired, and these individuals become "an exceedingly great army" for the Lord (vs. 10)! I can't help but think to myself when I read this account: *How many Christians have been slain by sexual sin?*

There are so many who have not taken their sins to the cross, repented, and then left them there. Satan likes to remind us of our past and whisper in our ears, "You made mistakes that you can never turn back from," and we seem to take those sins and put them in our backpacks to weigh us down throughout our lives. But Scripture tells us that Satan is an accuser and liar—because our Lord has promised that if we confess our sin, He who is able will forgive our sins and cleanse us from all unrighteousness (I John 1:7-9, Matthew 9:2 ). Jesus is the Lamb of God, and only He can take away our sin (John 1:29). **He died on that cross to cover all sin (I Corinthians 15:3, II Corinthians 5:15) so don't let Satan keep you down (James 4:7).**

**REMEMBER: MORE IS CAUGHT THAN IS TAUGHT!**

> *You are all sons of light and sons of the day. We are not of the night or of darkness. Therefore let us not sleep, as others do, but let us watch and be sober. - I Thessalonians 5:11*

**Suggested Resources:**

Kay Arthur, *The Truth about Sex*

Douglas Wilson, *Reforming Marriage*

Karen Lindwall-Bourg MA, LPC-S, FT, *Wellness: The Awareness of the Whole Individual*

Steve and Cathy Gallagher, *Create In Me a Pure Heart-Answers for Struggling Women*

Steve Gallagher, *At the Altar of Sexual Idolatry*

Jim Logan, *Reclaiming Surrendered Ground: Protecting Your Family from Spiritual Attacks*

Joshua Harris, *Not Even a Hint: Guarding Your Heart Against Lust*

Nancy Leigh DeMoss, *Lies Women Believe and the Truth that Sets Them Free*

Edward M. Smith, *Healing Life's Deepest Hurts*

Cynthia Spell Humbert, *Deceived by Shame, Desired by God*

Sandy Day, *Living in His Forgiveness: A Bible Study for Post Abortive Women*

Quin Sherrer and Ruthanne Garlock, *A Woman's Guide to Spiritual Warfare*

Waylon O. Ward, *Sex Matters: Men Winning the Battle*

# Chapter 2
# Tip 2
## Approach the Topic with Modesty!

*...and the parts that are unpresentable are treated with modesty.*
*– I Corinthians 12:23b (NIV)*

In the Prelude, I posed the questions: "How do you feel about giving your child the 'sex talk'? Are you dreading it?"

When I began this ministry 19 years ago as a result of seeing the curriculum being taught at my son's school, my objective was to awaken parents to the graphic content of the *Learning About Sex* education curriculum that was promoted as "Christ-centered" and "Bible-based." It had detailed pictures of naked male and female adults—along with a graphically worded description of sexual intercourse that included what went into what—for eight-year-old children to view!

At every parent meeting where I spoke, I asked a parent to read that description aloud, and not one of them ever could. They felt it would be "too embarrassing" to read aloud, and I found that very revealing.

Why is there discomfort in talking with our children about sex? The sex experts would say, "You just need to get over it," and then say something like, "You are too old-fashioned or too Victorian in your thinking, and you just need to get with the times." **I would propose to you that if you are uncomfortable with talking graphically about sex with your children, this is a natural and healthy response, because the graphic approach is not biblical.**

Did you know that God never mentions the genitals or the act in detail in scripture? I once asked Dr. Chris Mitchell, author of the *Song of Songs Concordia Commentary* and consultant for the *I Corinthians Commentary*, if I was interpreting the above scripture (I Corinthians 12:23b) correctly?[10] He verified that I was, and explained that God is modeling a tremendous amount of modesty for us in scripture. He went on to say that in Song of Songs, which is often called the "Bible's hot book on sex" by some ill-informed scholars, Solomon describes his wife's body in detail; but notice that Solomon skips the genital area.

> *How beautiful are your **feet** in sandals, O prince's daughter! The curves of your **thighs** are like jewels, the work of the hands of a skillful workman, your **navel** is a rounded goblet; it lacks no blended beverage. Your **waist** is a heap of wheat set about with lilies. - Song of Songs 7:1-2*

Dr. Mitchell went on to say that the genitals were considered such a holy, procreative area, that they were treated with a tremendous amount of modesty. In many of the antique books I have collected, I noticed the same trend; modesty was emphasized when talking to children.

For example, in one book from 1912, the author addresses a parent who "thinks that the way to protect her daughter of fourteen from possible danger is to tell her everything in detail."[11] The author replies:

> *To this mother I say, with renewed emphasis, that **information does not protect**. I would be extremely careful in what I said to a girl of fourteen. To "tell her everything in detail," as this mother suggests, might be to **put her in a place of great danger**. We must remember that, just at this period of her life, the creative forces of her being are receiving a new impulse. Not only are new powers awakening in her body, but in her mind as well. **Especially is her imagination increasing greatly in its activity, and is prone to follow any suggestion made**

---

[10] Dr. Chris Mitchell is the author of *The Song of Songs Commentary* published by Concordia Publishing House and he is a seminary professor at Concordia St. Louis Seminary for the Lutheran Church Missouri Synod.

[11] Mrs. Woodallen Chapman, *How Shall I Tell My Child*, Fleming H. Revell Co., New York, 1912, p.50

*to it along the line of this new process of development. And therein lies the danger of the plan this mother proposes.*[12] (emphasis added)

This author did not have years of research on what talking to kids about sex (sex education) would do to children, but I believe the Holy Spirit was speaking through this woman to give parents at the time tremendous insight. Another example of modesty comes from Dr. Mary Ries Melendy, a female physician who taught in 1904 under the heading "Sexual Organs are to be Kept Sacred":

*God made them [the sex organs], and they are the most sacred of all, for to them is given the honor and privilege, under right conditions, after marriage, of creating life.*[13]

In the 1990s, the **RSVP America** (Restoring Social Virtue and Purity) organization was instrumental in: bringing about an awareness of the error of Alfred Kinsey's "science"; exposing the bogus field of human sexuality based on Kinsey's fraudulent science; and proving that laws that once protected marriage, women, and children were removed because of reliance on Kinsey's "science." The authors of the RSVP America Training Manual well stated:

*Sex was once hidden out of recognition of its power as well as a sense of modesty and respect for privacy. What was once sacred is now, in the name of science and freedom, being taught as "safe sex" and sex education in public, private, and parochial school classrooms.*[14]

If you think this information through logically, would you show your child a picture of a Playboy centerfold or would you read an excerpt of the description of sexual intercourse from a trashy romance novel? I will assume your answered is an unequivocal "No!"

**The foundation for sex education has always been to focus on the act and the genitals, thereby removing any modesty that children would naturally have in this area. Children's modesty**

---

[12] Ibid, p. 51
[13] Mary Ries Melendy, M.D., *VIVILORE: The Pathway to Mental and Physical Perfection*, W.R. Vansant Pub, 1904, p.295
[14] Judith Reisman, Ph.D., Dennis Jerrard Ph.D., Colonel Ronald Ray U.S.M.C.R., and Eunice Ray, *RSVP America Training Manual*, First Principles, Inc., Crestwood, KY, 1996, p.4

**has to be removed in order to groom them for sex outside of marriage.** The pleasure of the act—to be experienced outside of marriage—is elevated; and one of the other main purposes for the act—procreation—is eliminated through the promotion of abortion, sodomy, and birth control.

Modesty is a standard given to us by God. He models it for us in His Word and encourages us to remain pure in our thoughts, words, and deeds (Psalm 119). If we take away modesty from children, hence opening them up to sexual sin, God has a few words to say to us about that:

> Whoever causes one of these little ones who believe in Me to sin, it would be better for him if a millstone were hung around his neck, and he were drowned in the depth of the sea. Woe to the world because of offenses! For offenses must come, but woe to that man by whom the offense comes. – Matthew 18:6-7

It is easy for us to see Planned Parenthood or the pornography industry leading our little ones to sin, but are there others who may be doing so? What about the Christian publishing companies who use writings from *experts* in sex education (those who believe in humanism, communism and eugenics); will they suffer that millstone? The ever more important question is: Have I as a parent unintentionally led my little one to sin?

Case in point: When receiving my sex education training (provided by SIECUS, the organization founded at the Kinsey Institute), to be qualified to teach in the schools, we went through what I thought at the time was an odd activity: we were asked to stand and recite the name for the male and female genitals out loud several times. This exercise, we were told, was designed to take away any modesty we had toward the subject. The rationale was that if we were no longer modest about these terms, we could then encourage the children to no longer be modest about these terms.

By the time I learned the biblical truth regarding this issue, I had already been following the instructions of the "experts": *teach them the correct anatomical terms for their genitals*. My response was to go to my children and apologize to them and to quickly change my terminology. (We will expand more on this in Tip #4). I began to be more modest in my approach.

The Barna Group recently conducted a study, in which they found that our current generation of young people believes that *not recycling their trash* is more morally wrong than *viewing pornography*.[15] Pornography is so widely accepted in society today, that many see nothing wrong with viewing others engaged in sex acts. I believe this is partially due to the effects of sex education on children. Once modesty is removed through sex education, it would be natural for kids to view pornography, because they have already been exposed to the act and the genitals. **Sex education, in the way it is designed, is pornography.**

In 1996 the Catholic community responded to the connection of sex education and sex stimulation in their informational booklet, *Parents and the Purity of Children*:

> *Pope Pius in his encyclical "On Chaste Wedlock," in 1930, warned against any type of (sex) education helping people to "sin subtly." Much of our dramatic presentations which are defended as "realistic" are really pandering to the sexual prurience, and tumescence-seeking of easily stirred children, adolescents, and adults... Sexological research and its application in science (as in sex education) and art are notorious for the seduction of the parent, teacher, lawyer, physician, psychiatrist, social worker, nun and priest.*[16]

Several years ago as I was uncovering the origins of the *Learning About Sex* series, I received a call from a Lutheran pastor. He was attempting to challenge the use of this series in the elementary school (grades first through eighth) associated with his church. While some parents supported his concern, others, along with a couple of teachers, presented strong opposition. This curriculum had been taught at this school for over thirty years, and this pastor shared that of all the congregations he had worked in, he had never seen more sexual sin than there was in this congregation. He believed that as a result of the exposure to explicit sexual information through the *LAS* series, many adults in their community, who were once taught the curriculum as youth, were involved in unhealthy sexual practices.

---

[15] http://www.heartlightministries.org/2016/10/your-son-and-porn/
[16] Rev. H. Vernon Sattler, C.Ss.R., PhD., *Parents and the Purity of Children*, Central Bureau, St. Louis, 1996,. 40-41

In addition, he told of a specific incident that occurred at his church which demonstrates the connection between sex education and pornography. The summer after an eighth grader graduated from this school, he broke into the school and accessed porn on the computers. You may ask, "Why did he go there to view porn?" I believe it was because this was where his modesty had been taken away to begin with. The school was where he was first sexually stimulated—by being exposed year after year, for eight years—to the act which was intended to be reserved for marriage.

**There is a huge connection between sex education and pornography, and it's time more parents and teachers understand this.**

If you use God's model of modesty when talking to your children, I guarantee you will not feel uncomfortable or squeamish at all!

**REMEMBER: APPROACH THE TOPIC WITH MODESTY!**

*As for God, His way is perfect; the word of the Lord is proven; He is a shield to all who trust in him. - Psalm 18:30*

**Suggested Resources**

**For children:**

Ami Loper, *The Miracle of Life* (for young children) and *The Miracle of Change* (for girls)

Jennie Bishop, *The Princess Kiss* and *The Squire and the Scroll*

Gary and Anne Marie Ezzo, "Reflections of Moral Innocence": a DVD program teaching parents how to teach chastity, purity, modesty, and self-control to their children

**For pre-teens:**

Dannah Gresh, *Secret Keeper: The Delicate Power of Modesty*

Tim and Ami Loper, *The Mission: Boy to Man* (Part 1 only, part 2 is for teens)

**For teens:**

Randy Alcorn, *The Purity Principle*

# Chapter 3
# Tip 3
## Identity Matters!

*But you are a chosen generation, a royal priesthood, a holy nation,
His own special people, that you may proclaim the praises of Him
who called you out of darkness into His marvelous light.*
*- I Peter 2:9*

It was no accident after prayer was removed from the public schools in 1962 and Bible reading removed in 1963—both Supreme Court decisions—that sex education was put into the schools in 1964 with the start-up of SIECUS. Teaching children about God had to be stopped first so they would no longer have the understanding that they were made in the image and likeness of Him (Genesis 1:27). Instead, they would be taught they were sexual beings capable of sexual acts.

**One of the most devastating results of talking to children about sex was that it gave children a sexual identity.** Children were introduced to the act that should be saved for marriage and the medical terminology for their genitals, removing all modesty on the subject. As a result, their minds were imprinted with something that had never been impressed on the children before—that they were sexual beings.

Secular child experts in the first half of the 20th century did not identify knowledge of sex and sexuality as a prime childhood need. Theorists Jean Piaget, Carl Rogers, Abraham Maslow, and B.F. Skinner concentrated on such individual and group skills as learning to reason, submitting to authority, moral thinking, task achievement, self-actualization, mutual cooperation, and social interaction as the child's major developmental objectives.[17]

It was Alfred Kinsey who was the first to suggest children were sexual from birth and capable of enjoying sexual pleasure, even infants.[18] Where did he get such data? We now know that he interviewed pedophiles who had raped children.[19] Sadly—based on the interviews of these pedophiles, who used stopwatches to time what they believed to be children's orgasms during intercourse—as a society we were led to believe that children are *sexual beings* who should be trained in how to handle their sexuality.[20]

Michael Balfour, researcher and author stated:

> [When] someone in public life can persuade enough people to act on the assumption that his interpretation is valid, he can so influence the character of the future as to make it consistent with his predictions.[21]

Believing that children are sexual from birth, changed everything:

- Schools were now faced with the dilemma of teaching children how to handle their *sexuality*.

  *As soon as it was established, SIECUS became a super-salesman for sex education. Soon after, schools began talking sex education.[22]*

- Legislatures were faced with looking at a sexual predator with more sympathy, hence reducing their sentences

---

[17] Michael Craven, "What is wrong with Sex Education," Center for Christ and Culture, January 16, 2008.
[18] Alfred Kinsey, *Sexual Behavior in the Human Male*, W. B. Saunders Company, Philadelphia, 1948, 180-181
[19] Judith Reisman, "Sexual Sabotage: How One Mad Scientist Unleashed a Plague or Corruption and Contagion on America," World Net Daily, Washington DC, 2010, p. 24
[20] Kinsey, *Sexual Behavior...* 175-181. Orgasm in infants is described as "sobbing, sometimes with an abundance of tears, and afflicted with 'extreme trembling,' collapse, and sometimes fainting." Kinsey also wrote that the children "enjoy the experience," although many "fight away from the partner."
[21] Michael Balfour, *Propaganda in War, 1939-1945, Organizations, Policies and Publics in Britain and Germany,* London, Routledge and Kegan Paul, 1979, p. 424
[22] Gloria Lentz, *Raping Our Children: The Sex Education Scandal*, Arlington House, New Rochelle, N.Y., 1972, p. 21

from imprisonment for life or the death penalty to being *therapeutically* managed and living in our neighborhoods:

> The sometimes extreme seductiveness of a young female is a factor which has no place in the law, but it certainly affects motivation. Even at the age of four or five, this seductiveness may be so powerful as to overwhelm the adult into committing the offense. The affair is therefore not always the result of the adult's aggression; **often the young female is the initiator and seducer**.[23] (emphasis added)

- Medical personnel were taught that if children are sexual beings, they must be interviewed separate from their parents so the doctor could get a clear picture of their sexual activity. Children must be given vaccines that prevent sexual diseases such as Hepatitis B and Human Papilloma Virus (HPV) because they are capable of intercourse at any time and unable to remain pure until marriage.

- Christian churches and schools were faced with the challenge of taking this new "science" and developing "Christian Sex Education" programs using scripture meshed with Kinsey's fraudulent data. One of the most popular of these programs rationalized the need to talk graphically with your kids about sex:

> The famous Kinsey reports are more specific. His study reveals that by the age of 20, 75% of males had premarital coitus. Of the women marrying for the first time between 16 and 20, 47% were no longer virgins.[24]

- Parents were confronted with the task of now talking graphically to their kids about sex, and because many found it uncomfortable, they either remained silent or relied on the schools and churches to do it. At the same time, sex education experts made clear their belief that parents were ill-equipped to teach their children accurately about sex. Past president of SIECUS, Dr. Harold Lief, had this to say:

---

[23] Slovenko, R. and Phillips, C. 1962, "Psychosexuality and the Criminal Law," *Vanderbilt Law Review*, Vol. 15, p. 809
[24] Erwin J. Kolb, *Parents Guide to Christian Conversation about Sex*, Concordia Publishing, St. Louis, MO, 1967, p.20

*Most parents are so damn anxious about this [sex education] that if they attempted to teach it, all they do is transfer their own anxiety to the kids. A lot of parents are so hung up about sex that their own repressive and suppressive mechanisms just increase their kids' guilt and anxiety. The parents who scream "let the parents do it" are just the ones who will stir up all kinds of harmful emotions in their children. They think they'll do a good job—but I doubt it.[25]*

Words and images are powerful. Sexual words and images are even more powerful; if you have ever viewed pornography or read trashy romance novels, you well know what I am talking about. Those who developed sex education came up with a way to convey sexual words and images to children, called the *SAR technique,* or Sexual Attitude Restructuring. The goal of this technique is to break down all modesty and reshape attitudes toward sexuality, as well as train the healthy brain to consider other sexual mores. Leading expert on Kinsey, Judith Reisman, reports:

*The neurochemical impact of sexualized media, whether commercial or educative, upon children's nascent brains, minds, and memories, is producing a new breed of children, hence a new breed of adults and a new type of society.[26]*

Judith Reisman later went on to report:

*Using a "Graffiti Board" to desensitize students to "dirty words," sex educators taught children about nudity, adolescent pregnancy, masturbation, abortion, homosexuality, contraception, divorce, group sex, and extramarital relations. By 1973, "Thanks to Kinsey, every form of deviance is promulgated throughout our schools," reported psychiatrist Charles Socarides, MD.[27]*

Today we have an evolving field of sex education that is focused on putting doubt in children's minds regarding their gender, even

---

[25] Gloria Lentz, Raping Our Children: The Sex Education Scandal, Arlington House, New Rochelle, N.Y., 1972, p. 165
[26] Judith Reisman, PhD., *Kinsey, Crimes, & Consequences*, The Institute for Media Education, Crestwood, KY, 2000, p.174
[27] Judith Reisman, "Sexual Sabotage...p. 183

though they are born male or female. Read the following example and see how children are being led down the path of questioning this at kindergarten level:

*When we are born, a doctor or midwife calls us boy or girl because of what we look like on the outside.* **They choose a word or label (usually boy or girl, or male or female) to describe our bodies.** *But that's based on our outside, our cover, and* **who they think we are.** *What about our whole body, inside and out?* **What about who we think we are?**[28] (emphasis added)

Another example of a suggested identity comes in the popular "Christian" sex education series, the *Learning About Sex* series that was advertised as a "Christ-centered, Bible-based" curriculum:

*Scientific study of homosexuality [i.e. Kinsey's "science"] is comparatively new and relatively unknown. It is estimated that about a third [Kinsey's statistic was 37%] of all males have had some homosexual experience at some point... Many young people experience homosexual attraction to people of their own age as well as to older or younger people...* **Most of us cannot escape homosexual temptations***, but homosexual practice involves choosing this pattern of action.*[29] (emphasis added)

We have an epidemic of youth who are declaring they are gay, and many adults don't understand where this is coming from. In her report titled, "Crafting Gay Children: An Inquiry into the Abuse of Vulnerable Youth via Government Schooling & Mainstream Media," Dr. Judith Reisman reveals how our children are being recruited into dangerous lifestyles:

*Sexuality philosophers like Gilbert Herdt, the editor of "Gay and Lesbian Youth," defines adult homosexuals (not bisexuals) as "coaches" and "guides," who help children overcome their heterosexual victim status by "coming out" into homosexuality. Protected by federal and state law, homosexual "guides" teaching "tolerance," "sexual diversity"*

---

[28] Cory Silverberg and Fiona Smyth, *Sex is a Funny Word*, Seven Stories Press, 2015, p.81
[29] Elmer Witt, *Life Can Be Sexual* of the *Learning About Sex* original series, Concordia Pub House, 1967, p. 44

*and such, frighten susceptible child audiences with Kinsey's "scientific" claim that, "at least one in ten of you are gay." Objectors are labeled "homophobic" fascists. Supporters are rewarded with love, approval and inspiring encouragement to be "gay and proud."[30]*

Dr. Reisman continues:

*Children, (labeled "initiates" as in prostitution or religion) are weaned from their "old fashioned" parents, first into a self-affirming semi-secret group, then by collective socialization into a "gay" cultural system (a form of cult).[31]*

Alfred Kinsey's "science" has been used to legalize all that *had* been illegal when America's laws were still based on the Bible; and those who encourage homosexuality have especially benefitted from it. Psychotherapist Edward Eichel, with M.A. in Human Sexuality, speaks of the benefits, he believes, of Kinsey:

*The objective of Kinsey-type programming is to change the concept of the family or "de-normalize" the heterosexual nuclear family. If you look to the statement of pedophile Theo Sanford, he said that if children could be weaned away from the nuclear family, they can then form emotional attachments with others beyond the family... With the systematic destruction of the family with a mother and father in it and with the family break-ups that are occurring, it is an opportune time.[32]*

Why is it so dangerous to give children a sexual identity? Why are many in the LGBTQ community so intent on encouraging children to consider an identity based on their sexuality above all other accomplishments? Why does Planned Parenthood devote the month of October to encouraging parents to talk to their kids about sex, hence employing the parents with the task of giving their children a sexual identity? Why is all of this a problem? Linda

---

[30] Judith Reisman, Ph.D., *Crafting "Gay" Children: An Inquiry into the Abuse of Vulnerable Youth via Government Schooling & Mainstream Media*, The Institute for Media Education, Crestwood, KY, 2000, p.18
[31] Ibid, p. 19
[32] Excerpt from the video "The Children of Table 34" distributed by The Family Research Council, 1998

Bartlett, author of *The Failure of Sex Education in the Church* summarizes this beautifully:

***It matters how we identify ourselves. If we are mistaken about our identity, we will be mistaken about our purpose, behavior, and choices.***[33]

Once a student is given that sexual identity—whether it be straight or gay—their purpose will not be to follow Christ, minister to the lost and hurting on this earth, or to help others to come to know Christ; it will be to pursue sexual pleasure and fight for all sexual rights to be legal. Dr. Miriam Grossman writes:

*Once kids believe that sexuality is "who they are," "their entire selves" from womb to tomb, the idea that it's an appetite in need of restraint makes little sense. And the notion of waiting years for the right time and person sounds irrational. Why restrain "who you are"? Why wait for "your entire self"? Couldn't that be unhealthy?*[34]

The choices children make once they embrace this *identity* will be to ignore the facts:

- that having more than one sex partner can put them in harm's way to contract diseases—some of which could kill them;[35]

- that aborting a baby not only kills an unborn child but causes many of those potential parents to suffer depression and emotional distress;

- that engaging in sodomy, an act God never intended the body to go through, can cause venereal diseases, cancers, and even death;[36]

- that to bear a child without a father to help protect and provide for the child means this child is more likely to grow up in poverty and repeat the cycle of having sex outside of marriage;[37]

---

[33] Linda Bartlett, *The Failure of Sex Education in the Church-Mistaken Identity, Compromised Purity*, Titus 2 for Life, Iowa Falls, IA, 2014, p.28
[34] Grossman, *You're Teaching My Child What?*, p. 29
[35] Please read *How Teen Sex is Killing Them* by Dr. Meg Meeker.
[36] See http://massresistance.org/docs/issues/homosexuality-health-book/index.html
[37] Patrick Fagan, "Social Stability in the United States" www.catholiceducation.org

- that any type of sexual activity outside of God's design can bring physical, spiritual, and emotional death.

I know this sounds dramatic and maybe old-fashioned to some today, but there was a time when divorce, out-of-wedlock pregnancy, venereal disease, and even suicide rates were low. **The Christian church influenced the culture with biblical values, and the family was recognized as a married man and woman with whatever number of children God chose to give them**; having numerous children was once looked upon as a blessing. We have drifted far from this norm very quickly over the past sixty years.

In an attempt to counter the onslaught of sex education programs that have been pouring into the schools, some well-meaning individuals came up with "abstinence" programs. At first, these programs promoted abstinence until marriage in a modest way. However, many abstinence programs today have evolved into sex education programs—explaining the act in detail and showing pictures of diseased genitals to students of all ages. There is a problem with this approach, as one blogger put it:

> *Abstinence says, "I must wait for sex until marriage." Purity says, "I don't have to wait to be the woman (or man) God created me to be." Abstinence says, "Because we are sexual beings, I must be cautious with the opposite sex." Purity says, "Because we are **persons** more than sexual beings, I can respect, talk to, learn from, work beside, and be patient with the opposite sex." Purity always journeys toward hope with the encouragement of the Holy Spirit. In fact, because of Jesus Christ, we can be restored to a life of purity even after we've failed to abstain.*[38] (emphasis added)

How can we raise up the next generation to believe, despite everything the media and schools are throwing at them, that they are made in the image of our Heavenly Father? How do we promote purity as the goal for which they should strive? God's Word is the answer!

We must stress to our children the following points:

- We are made in God's image (Genesis 1:27);

---

[38] Anna Mussmann is the editor of the blog "Sister, Daughter, Mother, Wife"

- We are His (Psalm 100:3);

- We are to be holy (I Peter 1:16);

- The Holy Spirit dwells within us (Galatians 6:15, II Corinthians 5:17) and gives us the power to turn away from evil! (Philippians 4:13);

- We are transformed through Christ Jesus! (Colossians 3:10);

- God defines biblical manhood and womanhood throughout the Bible (Gen. 2, Proverbs 31, Titus 2);

- We were once in the darkness, but in becoming a child of God, we walk into the light (Ephesians 5:8);

- Everything we do on earth, we are to do in the name of Jesus, giving all thanks to Him (Colossians 3:17).

If we can stress to our children their identity in Christ, we can counter any identity the world is throwing at them. Knowing who they are as God's children will influence the actions, decisions, and directions they take. Tim Tebow shared how important our identity can be in a recent interview:

> *Your identity is what you get to hold onto. It's the foundation of who you are. It's not what you do. You could put your identity into sports or your girlfriend or boyfriend or a job or even your family, but none of those are going to be an identity that sustains you through everything. What's going to sustain you is a relationship with Christ. That's going to give you the strength to get through everything else you go through in your life. My significance doesn't come in what the media says about me, what type of car I drive, what type of house I have, but it comes from who I am in Christ. Then I take that same framework and I get to apply that to everyone I come in contact with. You treat people with respect because they matter to God.*[39]

The world at this moment is trying to give our children a sexual identity. Children attending government schools, and even private

---

[39] Tim Tebow, The Testing of Tim Tebow, article in Decisions Magazine, November 2016 issue, pp. 32-33

and some Christian schools, are being taught that they can decide what is morally right or wrong for themselves.

Those who have been raped or molested often define themselves by these horrific experiences; some believe little of themselves or feel a tremendous amount of guilt for thinking they deserved it. Some, when raped by the same gender, then grow up believing that they must be "gay." I grieve for all the children who are being sexually abused daily, and I'm thankful that through the grace of God, all of them can be healed and restored! God provides amazing tools to help in this restoration through prayer and sound biblical counseling.

Through the sexual revolution, Satan has cast many lies, luring us to no longer embrace God's standard of purity and holiness, but rather focus on a sexual identity. Our enemy roams the earth seeking whom he can devour, but we have the power of God's Word to help our children flee from sexual immorality. Make sure you continue to remind your children who they are in Christ Jesus, because others are waiting in the wings to give your children a different identity—a sexual identity!

**REMEMBER: IDENTITY MATTERS!**

> *You are all sons of the light and sons of the day. We are not of the night nor of darkness. - I Thessalonians 5:5*

**Suggested Resources**

Tim and Ami Loper, *The Mission: Boy to Man*

Mabel Hale, *Beautiful Girlhood*

Staci McDonald, *Raising Maidens of Virtue*

Michael Farris, *How a Man Prepares His Daughter for Life*

Robert Lewis, *Raising a Modern-Day Knight: A Father's Role in Guiding His Son to Authentic Manhood*

Elisabeth Elliot, *Passion and Purity*

Linda Bartlett, *The Failure of Sex Education in the Church: Mistaken Identity, Compromised Purity*

Mike Cleveland, with Nathan and Jenna Wells. *Purity Challenge-Training Youth in the Battle for Purity*

# Chapter 4
# Tip 4
## Don't Use the "Sex" Word!

*Therefore a man shall leave his father and mother and be joined to his wife, and they shall become one flesh.*
*– Genesis 2:24*

When Noah Webster's dictionary of 70,000 words was released in 1828, it became the standard by which the citizens of this new nation, the United States of America, would have accurate knowledge and understanding of words derived from original language. He wanted "a national language as a bond of national union."[40]

Noah Webster understood language was a gift from God that had been bestowed to Adam in the very beginning of creation. Included in the introduction of the 1828 dictionary are references to the Tower of Babel event in the Bible and the confusion of language that occurred from that point on.[41] Webster researched for years all the Hebrew and Greek origins of words to make sure that we had the foundations of words. At that time, he only invented one new word: *demoralize*—which meant "to corrupt or undermine the morals of, to destroy or lessen the effect of moral principles on, to render corrupt in morals."[42]

---

[40] Rosalie J. Slater, "Noah Webster Founding Father of American Scholarship and Education," Foundation for American Christian Education, San Francisco, CA, 1995, p. 10
[41] Noah Webster, *American Dictionary of the English Language*, G. & C. Merriam Co., 1828, Introduction
[42] Rosalie J. Slater, "Noah Webster Founding Father of American Scholarship and Education," p. 10

Words have changed dramatically since the beginning of the sexual revolution. For example, take a look at the word "sex" when in it was defined in 1828 as:

> *The distinction between male and female; or that property or character by which an animal is male or female. The male sex is usually characterized by muscular strength, boldness, and firmness. The female is characterized by softness, sensibility, and modesty.*[43]

In 1935, Webster's dictionary still held to the original definition:

> *The physical distinction between male and female*[44]

After the launch of Alfred Kinsey's fraudulent scientific data through the release of his books, *Sexual Behavior and the Human Male* in 1948 and *Sexual Behavior in the Human Female* in 1953, the term "sex" took on an additional meaning:

> *1) either of the two divisions of organisms distinguished as male or female, 2) the character of being male or female, 3) **anything connected with sexual gratification or reproduction**; esp., the attraction of one sex for the other.*[45] (emphasis added)

Kinsey has succeeded, in large part, because today *sex* is commonly and unblushingly a topic of conversation.

If you use the term *sex*, what does that mean today? If you teach your children this term, what will it mean for them? *Sex* was defined based on God's Word, as in "male and female He created them" (Genesis 1:27). It encompasses a number of sinful acts, all condemned in Scripture. Even the United States Supreme Court Justice Ruth Bader Ginsburg commented on how confusing the term can be in today's culture, when she spoke to an audience at Columbia University School of Law:

---

[43] Noah Webster, *American Dictionary of the English Language*, (no page numbers given-alphabetical order)

[44] *New Handy Webster Dictionary*, The World Syndicate Publishing Co., New York, NY, 1935, p.424

[45] *Webster's New World Dictionary*, The World Publishing Co., Nashville, TN, 1974, p. 679

*Nine men [on the Supreme Court] hear that word, and their first associations are not what you want it to be....."Gender" as substitute for "sex" will ward off distracting associations.*[46]

What terms should parents use with their children? Where are we to search for such words? The answer is simple; we can look to God's Word to see what He has modeled for us.

*As for God, His way is perfect: the word of the Lord is tried: He is a buckler to all those who trust in Him. - Psalm 18:30*

As was stated in Tip #2: "Approaching the Topic with Modesty," nowhere in scripture does God use the term "sex." In the Bible we can read the terms: "know," "become one flesh," and "beget," which all relate to the procreative act between a husband and wife.

Another great resource to use is *Strong's Exhaustive Concordance of the Bible* where one can study the meaning of words in the original Hebrew and Greek. For example, according to the concordance:

1. *Chaste* is mentioned three times;

2. *Pure* and other forms of the word, (purely, pureness, purer, purify and purity) are mentioned 130 times;

3. *Sex, sexuality* and *sexual intercourse* are never mentioned once in God's Word.[47]

We can learn from this resource that "sex" is not God's word of choice on the subject of the intimate physical human relations, but rather "pure" and "chaste" are His standards. David tells us:

*How can a young man keep his way pure? By living according to your Word. - Psalm 119:9*

God repeatedly shows us, by His use of the terms, His desire for the Church to be chaste and pure. God's interest in purity and chastity lies in His being the Life Giver. Kinsey was preoccupied with sex and

---

[46] The Washington Times, "Ginsberg on Sex," November 23, 1993, p A5
[47] James Strong, *The New Strong's Exhaustive Concordance of the Bible,* Thomas Nelson Publishers: Nashville, TN., 1982, pp. 186 and 851.

sexuality because, for Kinsey and his perverted views, man alone was the life giver. He believed and taught that *anything goes,* and, as sexual beings, sexual expression must not be limited on any basis, for it is unhealthy to exercise moral self-government and be chaste and pure.

It is vital that we teach our children about chastity, purity, modesty, and self-control; all standards that God lays out for us in His Word. In our home, we used the term "marital act" to describe what God intended between a husband and wife. After apologizing to our young children for using the correct anatomical terms for the genitals, we switched to using the term "private parts," which stressed modesty and the fact that they were *private* and not to be shown to anyone other than mom or dad or the doctor, if needed.

You may be wondering how parents talked to their children about this subject prior to Kinsey and the birth of sex education. After searching through numerous antique stores to find books that addressed this subject, I was surprised to find out how simple it was back then. Their whole discussion revolved around "the flowers, the birds, and the bees." Communicating in such an indirect way preserved the child's modesty, avoided giving them a sexual identity, and displayed the modesty God exhibited in His Word. Let's look at a few examples of how God's life process was related from parent to child:

> She [the mother] may first tell you this beautiful truth, that all life comes from a tiny seed; that before you were born you were growing, just as the seed grows in the ground, or as the bird grows within the egg; that God so planned for your coming that He placed a sheltered nest for you within your mother's body... All human life comes from the father and mother; it is God's way of creating, and the most beautiful way that could be, because a child, having been a part of its parents' bodies, is the more dearly loved.[48]

What a beautiful indirect way of not only relaying God's life process but also stressing God's design for a mother and father to conceive and raise up the next generation. Here is another example of a

---

[48] Mary Ries Melendy, M.D., *VIVILORE-The Pathway to Mental & Physical Perfection,* W.R. Vansant Pub, 1904, p.291-292

parent explaining to a child God's design as is told in the chapter titled, "How You Came Here":

*After learning exactly how all the plant, fish, bird, and animal babies come into the world, I suppose you wonder how you got here yourself... You know that you are very different from animals. They have bodies, and life, and instinct, but they have no mind or soul, such as you have. It is because you have a mind and a soul that you are said to be made after God's own image... You heard, did you not, how the male and female bird found each other and how they agreed to make a dear little home for themselves and for their family? Well, when a man is quite grown up, when he is strong and well, and feels that he can earn enough to make a home, he begins to think about marrying, too. As he has a soul, he wants to find a wife with a soul like his, a wife whom he can love and trust. He looks around, and when he meets the right woman—the woman, who has a soul like his—he asks her to be his wife, and come and make a home for him. Then the two are married... At first, your family was a very small one, only father and mother... Mother knew that the souls of people (the masters of their little houses), are sent by God, to live in human bodies. Although she did not know what souls are made of—nobody does know that except God—she knew that the little houses in which they live and grow are made of food and air. Mother knew that in her body, just as in the body of all female animals, there was a little room with a tiny egg, so small that it could not be seen except with a microscope. Just like the bird's egg, it grew and changed as soon as some of father's life fluid got into it.[49]*

Did you notice that all *talks* went back to God's design and God's Life Process? God was at the center of families, and God's design for the family was the center point of *the talk,* not the act or the genitals. Another example shows Mrs. Woodallen Chapman giving the parent wisdom on how to tell their child:

*You see darling, father and mother are just two parts of a whole. A home isn't really complete, is it, unless there are both a father and a mother in it? You have to have a father to be*

---

[49] H.A. Guerber, *Yourself and Your House Wonderful*, The John C. Winston Co., Chicago, 1913, pp.260-263

*strong and brave and true; to take you fishing and to play ball with you, and to tell you about machinery. And then you have to have a mother to be tender and careful and loving; to sing songs to you, and to tell you stories; to kiss the bruised places, and to tuck you into your bed at night.*[50]

You will note in these examples that a family was described based on the first family in the Bible: Adam and Eve. When these books were written, the divorce rate was extremely low, the venereal disease rates were low, abortion, sex education and pornography were illegal, and the moral standard in the nation for a majority of adults was to wait until marriage. Fornication, sodomy, and sex education for children were never promoted. As you can see, we have come a long way in the past 100 years.

Spend time in God's Word and get to know His patterns in words and what standards He wants us to live by!

**REMEMBER: DON'T USE THE "SEX" WORD.**

*Now Adam knew Eve his wife, and she conceived and bore Cain, and said, "I have acquired a man from the Lord." Genesis 4:1*

### Suggested Resources

Gary and Anne Marie Ezzo, "Reflections of Moral Innocence": a DVD program teaching parents how to teach chastity, purity, modesty, and self-control to their children

Ami Loper, *The Miracle of Life* (for young children) and *The Miracle of Change* (for girls)

H.A. Guerber, *Yourself and Your House Wonderful*

---

[50] Mrs. Woodallen Chapman, *How Shall I Tell My Child*, Fleming H. Revell Co., New York, 1912, p.33

# Chapter 5
# Tip 5
## Teach Self-control

*People will be **lovers of themselves,** lovers of money, boastful, proud, abusive, disobedient to their parents, ungrateful, unholy, **without love**, unforgiving, slanderous, **without self-control**, brutal, not lovers of good, treacherous, rash, conceited, **lovers of pleasure** rather than lovers of God.*
*– 2 Timothy 3:2-4*

Many scholars today will tell you that there are no scriptures that directly address the topic of *masturbation*. However, we find in our current culture jokes being made about the act and movies that implant the idea in the minds of our youth and adults that this is normal and healthy. So historically, has this always been the standard? Once more, looking back to books written before the sexual revolution, I found that masturbation was once called "self-abuse."

Physician Dr. John Diggs shares a little history on the subject:

*Masturbation is the name given to sexual stimulation of oneself. Medical terminology of previous decades used the term "self-abuse." The term is not far off the mark if one considers that abuse of anything is the use of it in a manner not intended, or not reflecting, its nature. Badminton racquets are not designed to hit baseballs. This is abuse of the racquet.*

*Modern medical authorities and others frequently suggest masturbation as a manner of releasing sexual tension. This "masturbation-is-harmless" attitude was most famously endorsed by the fraudulent reports of one Alfred Kinsey in "Sexual Behavior in the Human Male" (1948), where he argued that repression of sexual desire was dangerous and unhealthy. Prior to that, the uniform opinion of physicians was reflected in the term "self-abuse."[51]*

Physician Mary Ries Melendy verifies what Dr. Diggs wrote and how this subject was addressed in 1904:

*The mind, as well as the body, is too often made the victim of self-abuse; and when it starts in the mind the habit is more than likely to extend to the body also... Not only does self-abuse ruin the health and the mind; but it so affects the appearance that, as a rule, all can tell what is the matter.[52]*

Let's address this topic from a practical point of view. Let's say a two-year-old boy is in the bathtub and his hand drifts down to his private parts. What is a parent to do? If we are to believe Kinsey—that children are sexual beings—then as a parent, you would never stop the child from exploring his sexuality. Lester Kirkendall—former President of the American Humanist Association, once on the board of Penthouse Forum, promoter of Kinsey's "science," associated with the Lucifer Trust, and co-founder of SIECUS[53]—advised parents on this subject by the Kinsey model:

*Attention to the genital parts comes and goes in various stages of the child's life. It is especially important in infancy that parents allow children to "grow through" this stage without giving it undue emphasis, without making the child feel that attention to his genitals is "bad" or forbidden.[54]*

*Also some children may masturbate, seek an outlet for physical and emotional tensions. Again, this is not abnormal.[55]*

---

[51] John Diggs M.D., article on "Masturbation" is displayed on The Matthew XVIII Group ministry website, http://www.matthewxviii.org/masterbation
[52] Mary Ries Melendy, M.D., *VIVILORE: The Pathway to Mental & Physical Perfection*, W.R. Vansant Pub, 1904, pp.294-295
[53] Claire Chambers, *The SIECUS Circle: A Humanist Revolution*, Western Islands, Belmont, MA, 1977, pp. 30–33 and 38
[54] Lester Kirkendall, *Helping Children Understand Sex*, Spencer Press Inc., Chicago, IL, 1952, p.10
[55] Ibid, p.23

The *Sex Information Education Council of the United States* published their guidelines in 1991 and has set the standards for how and what we are to teach children in the schools. Not surprising, based on Kinsey's model, masturbation has been promoted:

> **SIECUS**: *Key Concept 4: Sexual Behavior, Topic 1—Sexuality throughout Life, Level 1 (Age 5-8):* **it feels good to touch parts of the body.**

> **SIECUS**: *Key Concept 4: Sexual Behavior, Topic 2—Masturbation:* **Masturbation is often the first way a person experiences sexual pleasure**. *It is also stated that many boys and girls begin to masturbate for sexual pleasure during puberty.*[56] (emphasis added)

There are reasons why a young child's hand may go to this area. For example, when they are naked, the hand may find that area and explore simply because it is there; or if pants and/or diapers are too constricting, the hand may go there. If there is a urinary tract or yeast infection, the hand may also gravitate to this area. That does not mean children are in need of sexual release. The key here is not to overreact! When one of our children was younger, his hand gravitated to that area while in the bathtub. I gently took his hand and placed it on a toy, and thus I just simply redirected his activity.

In *How Shall I Tell My Child*, Mrs. Woodallen Chapman gives us wise counsel in the chapter titled, "When a Wrong Habit has been formed," written in 1912:

> *From the very first hour of its birth, the baby is being taught either **self-indulgence** or **self-control** through every experience of its daily life... She [a mother] can tell him or her of the sacredness of that part of the body, because it is connected with the bringing in of little children into the world, and the great need of guarding it carefully from all possible harm. Tell the child that those organs are as sensitive as the eye, and would be as greatly harmed by rubbing or other misuse as the eye would be.*[57] (emphasis added)

---

[56] National Guideline Task Force (SIECUS), *Guidelines for Comprehensive Sexuality Education*, Fulton Press, 1991
[57] Mrs. Woodallen Chapman, *How Shall I Tell My Child*, Fleming H. Revell Co., New York, 1912, 41-43

Despite the *sex experts*, who are not experts but predators wanting to train up your children to become self-indulgent sexual animals with no morals, we are to remain diligent at teaching our children self-control in this area. To ignore or encourage this action could cause addictions and worse. Authors Stephen Arterburn and Fred Stoeker list just some of the many problems associated with habitual masturbation:

* *Habitual masturbation consistently creates distance from God;*

* *Jesus said that lusting after women in your heart is the same as doing it. Since most masturbation involves a lustful fantasy or pornography, we're certain that nearly all instances violate Scripture;*

* *The pornography and fantasy that surround masturbation change the way we view women;*

* *Habitual masturbation is hard to stop. If you don't believe it, wait till you get married and try to quit masturbating;*

* *Masturbation is progressive. You're more likely to masturbate the day after you masturbate than you're likely to do it the day after you didn't. In other words, the pleasurable chemical reactions draw you to repeat the practice more and more. This is bondage, and God hates bondage in His sons.*[58]

I close this section with a few more wise words from Christian physician Dr. John Diggs:

> *It is very easy for teens to get into a habit of masturbation that precludes them from doing more productive things that will add to success in their lives. Masturbation is a dead end. It wastes time that could be dedicated to more productive pursuits. At the same time, the body is being trained to respond to self rather than a spouse. Sex is a physical and spiritual exchange between two people, a progressive bonding experience, and an expression of intimacy. The marriage will not endure if one is more interested in one's self than*

---

[58] Stephen Arterburn and Fred Stoeker, *Every Young Man's Battle*, Waterbrook Press, Colorado Springs, CO, 2002, p.109

*one's spouse. One does not have to be nice to the images in magazines or computer screens. No conversation, no exchange, no investment. No person. The risk is run that at some point fantasy will be preferred to reality.*[59]

## REMEMBER: TEACH SELF-CONTROL!

*The Lord God said, "It is **not good for the man to be alone**. I will make a helper suitable for him." - Genesis 2:18*

### Suggested Resources

Stephen Arterburn and Fred Stoeker, *Every Young Man's Battle*

Mrs. Woodallen Chapman, *How Shall I Tell My Child*

Gary and Anne Marie Ezzo, "Reflections of Moral Innocence": a DVD program for parents, teaching them how to promote chastity, purity, modesty, and self-control to their children

---

[59] John Diggs M.D., http://www.matthewxviii.org/masterbation

# Chapter 6
# Tip 6
## Foundations:
## Use the Bible to Talk with Your Children

*Your word is a lamp to my feet and a light to my path.*
*– Psalm 119:105*

After speaking to a group of church workers about the origins of sex education, its effects on children, and the urgent need for all of us to get back to God's Word, the children's minister, who was in attendance, had many questions and seemed enthusiastic about the information. Her husband, however, who was a pastor at another church, looked me in the eye and said with disgust, "Is that all? What about all the books on how to talk to your kids about sex? You mean to tell me, I'm to ignore all that and just use the Bible?"

We live in a time when the Bible is no longer the standard that people live by in America. Historically, in the 1800s, the Bible was the primary book used in schools; today it is banned. Our children are being exposed to more sexual immorality than ever before in our history.

We now have clear documentation that sex education was developed with the intent to minimize, if not remove, God's Word from our children—while not so subtly encouraging them to engage in sexual practices—which from a biblical perspective would be considered sin. The *American Association of Sex Educators, Counselors, and Therapists (AASECT)* was created in 1967 for teachers, health professionals and helping professionals. *AASECT* became the training ground for all sex educators in our country. Here is a chilling explanation of what they intended to do with our children through sex education:

> *AASECT's job is to provide sex information to the sex educator, train him/her in the psychotherapy techniques necessary to communicate this knowledge to others, and restructure his/her sexual values so as to equip him/her to expand their students' tolerance and acceptance of variant sexual practices and lifestyles.[60]*

**It is clear that those who developed sex education had the intent to shift us as a nation away from the culture of life, or God's design, to the culture of death, or Satan's schemes.** This could only be done if we walked away from God's Word and embraced man's science. Those who have worked diligently to deceive came up with brainwashing or indoctrination techniques for our children that have been extremely successful.[61] We are reminded in Ephesians who we are up against:

> *Finally, my brethren, be strong in the Lord and in the power of His might. Put on the whole armor of God that you may be able to stand against the wiles of the devil. For we wrestle not against flesh and blood, but against principalities, against powers, against the rulers of the darkness of this world, against spiritual hosts of wickedness in the heavenly places. - Ephesians 6:10-12*

God goes on further in Ephesians 6 to tell us how to battle this enemy with the full armor of God:

---

[60] *The State Factor*, "Restoring Legal Protections for Women and Children: A Historical Analysis of the States' Criminal Codes," by Dr. Linda Jeffery, April 2004, p. 5-7
[61] http://www.breitbart.com/big-government/2016/10/20/std-rates-united-states-reach-record-high/

1. The belt of **Truth** which allows you to stand firm against the enemy and frees up your movement to fight him (v 16). Satan comes at us with lies; we can counter punch with God's truth!;

2. The breastplate of **Righteousness** protects the heart, which is the centerpiece of the soul (v 14);

3. The shoes of the **Preparation of the Gospel of Peace;** God's Peace is needed in this crazy world (v 15);

4. The shield of **Faith** which extinguishes those fiery darts that Satan launches our way (v 16);

5. The helmet of **Salvation** which is our identity in Christ (v 17);

6. The **Sword of the Spirit**, which is the Word of God that can be used to slay the enemy (v 17)...

Are you noticing throughout these passages how important of God's Word is to us if we are to survive the enemy's attacks? The enemy is pouring lies and deception into this generation of children:

- "If it feels good do it."

- "There are no moral absolutes."

- "The Bible is old and doesn't apply to us today."

- "You can be whatever gender you want to be."

- "Whatever sex act you do or whatever you decide to dress up in defines who you are."

- "Try out every sexual lifestyle available and decide what you like."

- "Your rights and feelings trump the Bible and your responsibilities."

- "You can get rid of 'it' through abortion."

- "There is nothing wrong with watching porn."

- "If you love someone, it doesn't matter that you're a child and your partner is an adult."

...and the list goes on. This is why it is so vital that we study God's Word and teach it to our children.

God doesn't take this matter lightly. He states clearly that parents are to be teaching God's Word daily to their children:

> *You shall teach them to your children, speaking of them when you sit in your house, when you walk by the way, when you lie down, and when you rise up. And you shall write them on the door posts of your house and on your gates: that your days and the days of your children may be multiplied in the land of which the Lord swore to your fathers to give them, as the days of heavens upon the earth. - Deuteronomy 11: 19-21*

Using God's Word is so vital in the battle for our children's souls. Priscilla Shirer, Christian author and speaker, writes about the importance of the soul and how it is made up of four parts: your mind, your will, your emotions, and your conscience.[62] She then asked the readers in her Bible study to describe each part and discern how Satan targets them. Here is my analogy:

- **Mind**—God's thoughts (His Word) give us peace; Satan's thoughts give us fear, anger, worry, depression, doubt, and lust.

- **Will**—God gives us ambition to help others; Satan gives us ambition to focus on self and use others.

- **Emotion**—God can help us control our emotions and gives us compassion and love for others; Satan gives us volatile, out-of-control emotions that dictate actions without thought.

- **Conscience**—God gives us a clear moral compass in His word; Satan gives us "anything goes" and teaches us to ignore our conscience, which will become dull—or worse—hardened over time.

Priscilla goes on to share the following words of wisdom regarding the importance of following God's Word or directives for how we are to live:

---

[62] Priscilla Shirer, *The Armor of God*, LifeWay Press, Nashville, TN, 2015, p. 71.

*When you and I choose not to align our actions with God's truth—when we live in blatant rebellion against His will for us— we leave our heart exposed where Satan can take a clear shot.[63]*

I do not want Satan attacking my children, so it is vital that I teach my children God's Word! Here are some great lessons that God gives us through His Word so we can teach our children well:

- **Marriage**—The first holy institution recorded in the Bible is the marriage of one man Adam, to one woman Eve, in Genesis chapters 1 and 2. There are multiple accounts where having more than one wife doesn't bode well for the husband (Jacob and his bickering wives, in Genesis chapters 29 and 30, Solomon and his wives, in I Kings 10:3-4). There are no accounts of any other type of marriage in the Bible.

- **God's life process**—Adam *knew* his wife, and generations began in Genesis chapter 4. God models modesty in using the verbiage *to know* and *generations* throughout scripture.

- **Purity**—As was stated in a previous chapter, in *Strong's Exhaustive Concordance of the Bible, chaste* is mentioned three times; and *pure, purely, pureness, purer, purify* or *purity* are mentioned 130 times.[64] It is worth the time to study the word *purity* and how it is used in each case in the Bible.

  *How can a young man cleanse his way? By taking heed according to Your Word. - Psalm 119:9*

As parents, we need to direct our pre-teens and teenagers— depending on their level of maturity—toward God's ideal for them, and away from Satan's schemes.

- **Pornography**

  - **Proverbs 6 and 7:** Here is a message about the seductive woman and the naïve man. The man allowed the woman to eventually lead him to his death. Pornography is that seductive woman!

---

[63] Ibid
[64] James Strong, *The New Strong's Exhaustive Concordance of the Bible,* Thomas Nelson Publishers: Nashville, TN., 1982, pp. 186 and 851.

- **Job 31:1** is the account where Job shields his eyes so that he doesn't look lustfully on a young woman.

- **I Corinthians 6:18** encourages us to flee from all sexual immorality. Anything outside of the marital act is sexual immorality. **Fleeing** is the key here, and we are not to stay or tarry for awhile.

- **Psalm 101:4** talks about setting nothing wicked before our eyes.

- **Philippians 4:13** reminds us that with Christ we have the power to overcome any temptation put before us.

- **The standard for treating the opposite gender:** Our pre-teen sons were taught the scripture I Timothy 5:1 in which Paul exhorts Timothy to treat all young women as "sisters, with all purity." As our sons observed the dating world and how many of their peers act toward one another, they realized that most young men weren't looking at young women as sisters in Christ` or helping to keep them pure.

- **The difference between biblical love and lust:** When speaking to young adults, I write out a list of the characteristics of biblical love as stated in 1 Corinthians 13 and then ask the students to list the opposite characteristics, which provides them with a good picture of what lust is. If they are in a relationship, this exercise often helps them realize that the relationship is not based on being **in love** but **in lust**. On the next page you will see what this exercise would look like.

| BIBLICAL LOVE | LUST |
|---|---|
| Patient | In a hurry |
| Kind | Unkind |
| Not envious | Wanting what others have |
| Not boastful | Bragging |
| Not proud | Calling attention to self |
| Polite | Rude, not concerned with partner |
| Not self-seeking | Focus on self |
| Slow to anger | A time bomb of emotions |
| Keeping no record of wrongs | Keeping score |
| Telling the truth | Lies |
| Protective | Putting partner at risk |
| Filled with hope | Filled with doubt |
| Lasting | Momentary, never satisfied |

In the movie *Monumental*, Kirk Cameron interviews David Barton, a Christian historian, regarding our Christian foundations in America. David shared that our founding fathers thought the Bible was so vital to the stability of our nation, Congress issued a copy for every family in the thirteen colonies.[65]

Spend time in God's Word; get to know it well and teach your children how to use it so they can be equipped to counter the devil's schemes.

---

[65] *Monumental: In Search of America's National Treasure* by Kirk Cameron is available through Amazon.

**REMEMBER: USE THE BIBLE WHEN TALKING TO YOUR CHILDREN ABOUT GOD'S LIFE PROCESS!**

*For though we walk in the flesh, we do not war after the flesh: For the weapons of our warfare are not carnal, but mighty through God to the pulling down of strongholds: casting down imaginations, and every high thing that exalteth itself against the knowledge of God, and **bringing into captivity every thought to the obedience of Christ.*** *- II Corinthians 10:3-5*

**Suggested Resources**

*The Holy Bible*—My favorite is the King James Version (KJV).

*American Dictionary of the English Language, Noah Webster 1828* is helpful when using the KJV of the Bible understand the words used in 1611, or you can use the New King James Version (NKJV), which is written with more contemporary language.

James Strong, *The Exhaustive Concordance of the Bible* (1890), Cincinnati: Jennings & Graham

Robert Young, *Young's Analytical Concordance to the Bible*

Kara Durbin, *Parenting with Scripture: A Topical Guide for Teachable Moments*

Chuck Swindoll, *Searching the Scriptures: Find the Nourishment Your Soul Needs*

Kay Arthur, *How to Study Your Bible*

Kay Arthur and Janna Arndt, *How to Study Your Bible for Kids*

Lee Strobel, *The Case for Christ*

Dr. Robert G. Witty, *The Bible: Fact or Fiction*

Stephen Leston, *The Bible in World History-Putting Scripture into a Global Context*

Leland Ryken, *The Word of God in English-Criteria for Excellence in Bible Translation*

Rose Publishing, Inc., *Rose Book of Bible Charts, Maps & Timelines*

# Chapter 7
# Tip 7
## When Your Child Asks You Questions about Sex, Ask Them More Questions First

*When I was a child, I spoke as a child, I understood as a child, I thought as a child; but when I became a man, I put away childish things.*
*– I Corinthians 13:11*

Most parents avoid "the talk," until one day they find themselves in a crisis; their child comes to them with the big question, "Where did I come from?" First of all the *sex experts* would chastise you for not giving "the talk" earlier. They will then prompt you to believe, "This is it....my child wants to know all about sex, how conception occurs, and sexual attraction." Take a deep breath and remember these are children, not adults you are talking to!

As a school nurse, I taught many sex education classes, and I can tell you that if you give the above information, the usual response is a stunned look or a "yuck" or "that is gross" comment from the child. So remembering Tip #2, which was "Approach the topic with modesty," there is a different approach you can take with your child.

First of all, ask more questions first. For example, "Where did I come from" could mean "What state was I born in?" **Children are not sexual from birth and they are usually not hungry for sexual knowledge.** If a child is asking many detailed or graphic questions, please know that children are not born with this knowledge. There had to be a source for any graphic sex information they have. Were they exposed to sex education in a school or church? Were they exposed to pornography, or worse, sexual abuse by another child or adult? It is imperative that you explore further what your child does know and where they got that information.

I once had a conversation with one of my sons when he was in second grade. He was taking a bath, and I popped my head in to make sure he was okay. Evidently, he thought this was a good opportunity to ask me a question about some graphic information he had heard from a classmate at school. Being a nurse, I could have easily brought out the anatomy books and shown him pictures of the genitals and gone over all the *stuff* that he had heard. Thankfully, this situation occurred after years of research, and I was well aware that this would be the exact approach that Planned Parenthood and the porn industry would have wanted me to use. By now I also knew that their way wasn't a biblical approach, so I took a different tack. The conversation went something like this:

*Me:* Do you remember when we talked about the flower and how God designed the life process for all plants, animals, and people? (This took his mind away from any graphic information that was in his head and to a morally neutral object: the flower).

*Son:* I remember, Mom.

*Me:* Did you know that the marital act is such a special gift reserved only for a husband and his wife that God doesn't even mention it in scripture?

*Son:* No, I didn't know that.

*Me:* Since it is a gift God intended for marriage, just like a birthday or Christmas gift, God doesn't want that gift opened until the right time, when a man and woman are married. And He also wants you, me, and others to be modest with our words and conversations; meaning that this is not something to be talked about with classmates but is intended for the husband and the wife to talk about when they are married.

My son was relieved as I gave him some general information about God's life process, put it in the context of why God designed it, and taught a lesson of modesty—by also taking care to be modest in the words I used. I didn't give him information that he was never intended to handle.

Another example is from a friend of mine who told me the following story about her son when he was young. The conversation was between her son and husband, and it provides a beautiful example of how to talk to kids when questions arise; I asked her to write it down. Here is her account in her own words:

*Our son was taking Catechism, and the topic of adultery and premarital sex came up in the reading. This is a story about how the Holy Spirit gave my husband John the wisdom to respond to this reading and still keep our son innocent.*

*John prayed before talking to Joshua. When he went in to speak to Joshua, he still had no idea what he was going to say. God is so good, and this is what transpired: John told Joshua, "There is a special gift that God gives a husband and a wife to share after they are married. Adultery is when a couple shares this gift and they are not married.*

*"Let me give you an example about this gift. Let's say that you saved money up for a whole year to buy your brother Tim a bike. You bought the bike and hid it in the basement. The next morning you saw Tim riding the bike. How would that make you feel?" He naturally said that he would feel pretty bad. "Tim opened the gift before he was supposed to," John told Joshua. "That's what people do when they open God's gift before they are supposed to."*

*Joshua said to his dad, "But I don't even know what that gift is." John's response: "Okay, let's say you bought Tim a bike and you told me everything about the bike: the color, how many speeds, etc. How would you feel if I went and told Tim every detail about the bike? Would that spoil the gift?" Joshua said that it would. John then said, "That is why I do not feel I should explain to you in detail about this special gift that God gives a husband and a wife. I would ruin the preciousness of the gift. You have to trust me on this."*

*Joshua understood, and he has no desire to hear about sex from others because he doesn't want to spoil the gift. He is still innocent and God is so good. He put those words in John's mouth. God will honor those who seek His will and His way for our lives.*

The key to this story is that John *prayed* for wisdom before talking to his son. How many times do we pray before we act? In today's culture it is vital that we remember to turn to God for wisdom.

**REMEMBER: WHEN YOUR CHILD ASKS YOU QUESTIONS ABOUT SEX, ASK THEM MORE QUESTIONS FIRST!**

*Call upon me in the day of trouble; I will deliver you, and you shall glorify Me. - Psalm 50:15*

# Chapter 8
# Tip 8
## Look at Children through Jesus' Eyes and Not the Human Sexuality Experts' Eyes

*Then He took a little child and set him in the midst of them. And when He had taken him in His arms, He said to them, "Whoever receives one of these little children in My name receives Me: and whoever receives Me, receives not Me but Him who sent Me."*
*– Mark 9:36-37*

One of my favorite pictures hanging in our young son's room is of Jesus holding a young child and surrounded by other young children. Jesus viewed children as precious, innocent, and free from evil ambition. As a parent, I'm sure you have many fond memories of the cute things your child has said or done. And what a blessing that they are oblivious to all the stresses and evil things we are aware of today.

Jesus also believed that children were vulnerable and needed to be protected. He gave a warning for anyone who would try to corrupt a child or lead them to sin:

*Whoever causes one of these little ones who believe in Me to sin, it would be better for him if a millstone were hung around his neck and he were drowned in the depth of the sea.*
*- Matthew 18:6*

For far too long, these so-called experts have attempted to lead our little ones into sexual sin, and according to this scripture, they will meet with a very harsh judgment. One commentator explains the severity of this crime:

*This word makes a wall of fire about them [children]; he that touches them touches the apple of God's eye.*[66]

You can decide for yourself where Alfred Kinsey fits into this picture, but according to his interviews with pedophiles—those who had raped children—he came up with some chilling conclusions:

*...it must be accepted as a fact that at least some and probably a high proportion of the infant and older pre-adolescent males are capable of specific sexual response to the point of complete orgasm, whenever a sufficient stimulation is provided.*[67]

Along with the help of other academic elites and the media, Kinsey convinced the public he was *the authority* on sexuality, that children were sexual from birth, and that we needed to see children through his eyes, not through the eyes of Jesus. Amazingly, despite the questionable statistics Kinsey gathered, even the Christian church embraced his ideas. The following is a quote from a *research team* of conservative Christian pastors in the Lutheran Church:

*...Alfred C. Kinsey and his associates were discovering some facts about sexual behavior. Though many doubts have been expressed, both in the press and elsewhere as to the validity of the Kinsey findings, it is probably fair to say that, insofar as statistical studies can give us accurate information, the Kinsey books are reliable for the type of study made.*[68]

---

[66] Matthew Henry, *Matthew Henry's Commentary, Vol. 5*, Hendrickson Publishers, U.S.A., 1991, p. 205
[67] Alfred Kinsey, *Sexual Behavior in the Human Male*, W.B. Saunders Company, Philadelphia, 1948, p. 181
[68] Oscar Feucht, *Sex and the Church*, Concordia Publishing House, St. Louis, 1961, p. 7

The *research* done by these church leaders began a movement to develop something that had never been done in the entire history of the Lutheran Church: *Christian sex education.* The *Learning About Sex* series was developed, and several works cited in the bibliography of the series refer to Kinsey's book. Our parents were taught to look at children through Kinsey's eyes, and the sex education movement was off to a big start.

As previously discussed, most parents believe their children need to have the "sex talk" but feel uncomfortable. I once asked Dr. Judith Reisman, one of the leading experts on Kinsey, why parents seem to have this discomfort. She thought for a moment and said, "Audrey, *once adults talk to their kids about sex, they sexualize them to themselves, to adults, and to each other."* A lightbulb went off in my head: if we are the body of Christ and the Holy Spirit lives within us, that discomfort we feel is coming from God. **God never intended for parents to sexualize their children; they are to protect them!**

There are many sex experts that have come after Kinsey: Masters and Johnson, Lester Kirkendall, Mary Calderone, William Genne, Clark Vincent, Harriet Pilpel, Alan Guttmacher, Ralph Eckert, Evelyn Duvall, Ann Landers, William Cole, Donald Kuhn, James Hymes, James Pike, Karl De Schweinitz, Lester Beck, and Ira Rubin, among others. Not only were they dedicated to promoting Kinsey's view of human sexuality, most are listed in the *Learning About Sex* sex education series for children. Our parents didn't stand a chance at blocking sex education from entering the schools—because once the church leaders were deceived, they went on to lead their flocks to the slaughter.

**The only way that sex education can be eliminated is when parents no longer look at their children through the *human sexuality experts'* eyes and start looking at them through the eyes of Jesus.** For the younger parents of today, while your grandparents and great grandparents may not have been aware of the biblical narrative of Jesus, this is the way they viewed children—they need to be protected.

**Leaders in the church are also going to have to shift their point of view about children.** For example, many Christian groups are cropping up to combat sex education and pornography, and I highly commend them for that. However, I recently was part of an on-line event to help parents when dealing with pornography and their kids. The answers provided were actually directing the parents to use the very techniques that Kinsey promoted; talking directly and graphically with their kids about sex.

**Remember, we have a much better tool to combat pornography— God's Word.** If we can look at our children through Jesus' eyes, we can be motivated to protect them by providing information with a very modest approach, such as *the flower, the birds, and the bees* talk.

After every seminar I present I always take time for Q & A. While some parents ask questions openly, others wait until everyone has left. That was the case recently, when a mother approached me and asked a question that literally took my breath away. She explained that she had just adopted two sisters, two- and four-years-old, who had been rescued from sex trafficking; they were put in rooms with men who could do whatever they wanted with them. This mother then asked, "How do I talk to my girls about sex, because they already know what it is?"

Taking a deep breath, I quietly prayed for wisdom. After a brief pause, I explained to this mom that her daughters did not know God's beautiful plan but had experienced Satan's plan of lust and devastation. I reminded her that these precious babies are beautiful, holy, and still innocent in the eyes of Jesus. I encouraged her to teach her girls about God's plan and what chastity and purity look like. I encouraged her to start looking at them through Jesus' eyes, not through the eyes of Kinsey or the world. Let us all do the same!

**REMEMBER: LOOK AT CHILDREN THROUGH JESUS' EYES AND NOT THE HUMAN SEXUALITY EXPERTS' EYES.**

*Then they brought little children to Him, that He might touch them; but the disciples rebuked those who brought them. But when Jesus saw it, He was greatly displeased and said to them, "Let the little children come to Me, and do not forbid them; for of such is the kingdom of God." - Mark 10: 13-14*

**Suggested Resources**

Jennie Bishop, *The Princess and the Kiss* and *The Squire and the Scroll*

Randy Alcorn, *The Purity Principle*

Linda Bartlett, *The Failure of Sex Education in the Church*

Judith Reisman, *Sexual Sabotage*

Dr. Miriam Grossman, *Unprotected*

Karen Booth, *Forgetting How to Blush*

# Chapter 9
# Tip 9
## We Want Our Children to be Morally Innocent, but Not Naïve

*That we should no longer be children tossed to and fro and carried about with every wind of doctrine, by the trickery of men, in the cunning craftiness of deceitful plotting.*
*– Ephesians 4:14*

The year was 1997. I had been asked to serve on the curriculum review committee for the sex education curriculum at the Lutheran school where my oldest son was attending. That curriculum was the *Learning About Sex* series. At that time I only knew a thimbleful of the information about sex education compared to what I now know. I asked the principal if he could give me fifteen minutes of our meeting to explain why I thought Alfred Kinsey's "science" was in the *LAS* series.

Honestly, that was the most intense fifteen minutes I had ever endured. Not only was it difficult to speak, but once it was over, I was physically exhausted. It was only later that I realized what a great spiritual battle had just taken place. One male teacher reacted angrily and growled, "Why you, why now? The LAS Series has been in Lutheran schools for 30 years; why didn't any Lutheran pastor or teacher find this error?" He then went on to tell us that he had not been given any information as a child and was embarrassed horribly by the guys in the locker room in his school.

While this gentleman's embarrassment was genuine, and while we do want our children to be morally innocent, we do not want them to be naïve. By this I mean that we are not to ignore this issue or give them no information (which makes them naïve or ignorant of some information they will need); but the way in which we present the information can still maintain their moral innocence. If I go over the act in detail and show graphic pictures with children, they are no longer morally innocent about sex. Their senses will be on high alert when they hear a reference to the genitals or the act. They will be reminded of those graphic words or pictures every time.

**However, if we use the flowers, birds and bees to talk about God's life process with our children, we can still maintain their moral innocence. As a matter of fact, their moral innocence can actually protect them from the graphic world around them.** Let me give you a personal life example:

When our firstborn son was twelve-years-old, our second son was ten, and our daughter was nine, they were in the back seat of our car while my husband drove them home from school. While at a stoplight my husband heard the kids say, "Dad, look, there's a naked woman!" Abruptly, my husband turned around, thinking there was a naked woman running around in traffic. He was saddened to see that a jeep full of teen boys a few cars away had opened a *Playboy* centerfold and put it to the window for the children to see.

My husband responded to the children by saying, "Kids, turn away— that's not appropriate," which is a fabulous lesson for any father to give to their children! As they drove away, my oldest son said to my husband, "Dad, she was not naked, she had on black underpants." You see, my son had never seen a picture of a naked woman before and since he had no other reference, he went to something his mind would know: a covered area = black underpants. His innocence protected him from what he had seen.

Another example is given by Gary Ezzo in the video series, "Reflections of Moral Innocence." Gary shared a story, related to him by the mother of a five-year-old boy returning home after his morning in Kindergarten. There was a speaker that day who had come in to talk to the children about HIV and AIDS. Horrified at what her child might have been exposed to, she asked her son what he learned. His reply was, "Something about when we come to an *intersection* we are supposed to have a *condo*." Again, this child went to something he knew, which was **intersection** and not **intercourse,** and **condo** instead of **condom**.

Dr. Miriam Grossman shares why children respond this way:

> *A young child's ability to think logically is limited. His understanding of the world is magical and egocentric. Why did his uncle leave? Because little Johnny wished he would. Why is it raining? So Johnny can wear his new boots. He devises his own theories to explain reality, based on his experiences. Providing facts that are beyond his experience—his uncle had a heart attack and went to the hospital; it's raining because ocean water evaporates...will likely be ineffective. They will sound bizarre, even impossible, to him. The result: confusion.*
>
> *The sex ed oligarchy must realize that a young child has his own theories about where babies come from, and he will cling to them regardless of how carefully and deliberately parents follow their instructions. Large amounts of unexpected information that cannot be easily assimilated into previously held beliefs can be distressing to children.*[69]

In the 1980s, when HIV/AIDS was discovered in the gay community, the *sex ed oligarchy* rationalized that they needed to go to the children in the schools and teach them about every type of sex act imaginable. In the 1990s we had the explosion of the rape culture, which is directly related to the explosion of pornography industry; and now sex educators are talking to kids about how to say "no" and when to give consent (notice they don't teach children abstinence). Since the U.S. Supreme Court decision in 2015 to legalize gay marriage, children are now being bombarded with the LGBTQ lifestyle. They are even being encouraged to deny every cell in their bodies that tells them they are one gender, and to consider taking steroids and mutilating their bodies to "become" a different gender.

Here is another example of the beauty of keeping children morally innocent but not naïve: In the spring of 2000, my five-year-old daughter, with several little friends, bent down to look at the tulips that were blooming. I was standing behind her with the other moms, when my daughter proceeded to tell the girls the story of the flower

---

[69] Miriam Grossman, M.D., *You're Teaching My Child What?*, Regency Publishing, Inc., Washington D.C., 2009, p. 30

and how it had a mommy part and a daddy part and when the two got together a baby flower is made. The other mothers and I just smiled as we looked at these morally innocent children and saw a picture of God. Now, had my daughter been giving the graphic talk to her little friends at that moment, that scene would have taken on a different tone. **I say, let's let children be children for as long as possible!**

**REMEMBER: WE WANT OUR CHILDREN TO BE MORALLY INNOCENT, BUT NOT NAÏVE!**

> *...but I want you to be wise in what is good, and simple concerning evil. - Romans 16:19b*

**Suggested Resources**

Gary and Anne Marie Ezzo, "Reflections of Moral Innocence" DVD series

# Chapter 10
# Tip 10
## The Sexual Revolution Can Continue With Our Children or It Can End With Our Children

*And I looked, and arose and said to the nobles, to the leaders, and to the rest of the people, "Do not be afraid of them. Remember the Lord, great and awesome, and fight for your brethren, your sons, your daughters, your wives, and your houses.*
*– Nehemiah 4:14*

We have come to the final tip, the final chapter, and I believe this tip is really a rallying cry. As addressed in the introduction, while doing my research on sex education, I learned much about the sexual revolution, and that is when I realized where the big push for sex education began. I imagine you probably read this book in hopes of receiving some sort of guidance on how to approach the topic of sex with your children—and hopefully you did; but I hope you learned a lot more. At this point, it is critical that you understand what is at stake here. I know the contents of this book is tough information to digest, so let's have a little history lesson to present the bigger picture.

At one time, America was considered a Christian nation. It wasn't because we had more Christians or more Christian churches than any other religion. We were a Christian nation because our laws and our government were founded on the principles of the Old and New Testaments.[70] Those who opposed Christianity and the Bible did not like this fact.

There are numerous biblical accounts demonstrating how easily God's people could be led astray as a result of sexual immorality. During my research I was stunned to learn that there was actually a plan to shift America away from our biblical principles. In his book, *Foundations: Their Power and Influence*, René Wormser, counsel to the U.S. Congressional Reece Committee in the 1950s, writes how the wealthy elite in our nation—the Fords, Carnegies, and Rockefellers—used their non-profit foundations to shape America into their vision, which was anti-biblical:

> An *"elite"* has thus emerged, in control of gigantic financial resources operating outside of our democratic process, which is willing and able to shape the future of this nation and of mankind in the image of ***its own value concept***.[71] (emphasis added)

What value concept were these philanthropic foundations intent on pushing upon Americans? This is easily determined by looking at the individuals and organizations these foundations funded. Here are just a few:

- Margaret Sanger believed in eugenics and promoted population control through birth control and abortion.

- Alfred Kinsey was considered the father of the sexual revolution, coined the phrase "Children are sexual from birth" and his fraudulent science was used as the justification for changes in the *Sex Offense* sections of the individual state laws. Kinsey promoted fornication, sodomy, bestiality, and pedophilia as normal and healthy sexual outlets to improve one's quality of life—especially one's sex life.

- The American Law Institute has worked diligently since 1923 to eliminate laws in the *Sex Offense* sections of state laws that once

---

[70] A.M. Dershowitz, *The Genesis of Justice: Ten Stories of Biblical Injustice that Lead to the Ten Commandments* 2000, NY: Warner Books
[71] René Wormser, *FOUNDATIONS: Their Power and Influence*, The Devin-Adair Company, New York, 1958, vii-xiii

protected marriage, women, and children. Of the thirty-five states reviewed by RSVP America, all used Kinsey's fraudulent science as the basis to gut any laws based on God's Word and offer up new laws that weren't so *repressive*, according to The Model Penal Code.[72] (italics added)

Through the work of individuals and organizations committed to ushering in humanism, communism, and eugenics, the sexual revolution actually began many years before the 1960s. In order to shift a nation away from God's standards, the following had to be weakened first:

1. **Marriage**, because it is the foundation of the family. This was done through the legalization of fornication, adultery, sodomy, and no-fault divorce.[73]

2. **Men**, because they are the heads of their families and the protectors. This was done by legalizing pornography in the 1950s which persuaded men to move away from love and protection to recreational sex. Men became playboys and women became objects of lust to be used.[74]

3. **Children**, so they would become a generation that believed they were sexual beings. This was done through sex education.[75]

This was a well-thought-out plan that was carried out by just a few individuals who were dedicated to creating moral chaos.[76] Sex education was an important tool used to accomplish this task. One of the most famous communist leaders in Russia, Joseph Stalin, understood the pillars of America's strength, hence what needed to be undermined:

---

[72] Dr. Linda Jeffery, *Restoring Legal Protections for Women and Children: A Historical Analysis of the State's Criminal Codes,* American Legislative Exchange Council-The State Factor, April 2004, 1-14

[73] RSVP Training Manual, 1-30

[74] Judith Reisman, Ph.D., *"Soft Porn" Plays Hardball; Its Tragic Effects on Women, Children,* and *the Family,* Huntington House Publishers, Lafayette, LA, 1991

[75] RSVP Training Manual,. 1-30.

[76] Three books that are recommended: *Kinsey: Crimes and Consequences* by Judith Reisman PhD; *R.S.V.P. America: Restoring Social Virtue and Purity to America* Handbook by Eunice Ray, Colonel Ronald Ray, Judith Reisman PhD, and Dennis Jerrard, PhD; *The SIECUS Circle* by Claire Chambers; and *FOUNDATIONS: Their Power and Influence* by René A. Wormser.

*America is like a healthy body and its resistance is threefold; its patriotism, its morality, and its spiritual life. If we can undermine these three areas, America will collapse from within.*[77]

Why would I ask you to believe that sex education or teaching children about their sexuality could contribute to the downfall of our nation? The following quote is from a reporter and mom who was concerned with the outcome of sex education in 1972, when at that time sex education had only been in the schools "officially" for 8 years (SIECUS was launched in 1964):

*If you are just the least bit upset about what sex education has produced so far, think what sex education will be like in the next ten or twenty years with the churches rapidly embracing the new sexual mores...*

*I suppose if enough religious leaders throw out the Bible, the Ten Commandments, and their own convictions, the prophecy in one of the sex education movies will doubtless materialize and the children will get the message: **"By the year 2000 there will be no more organized religion."** I hope that by now you are asking yourself why such a comment on religion appears in a sex education movie. I'll leave you to puzzle that one out for yourself. The same movie, incidentally, which is part of the Time of Your Life Series, **also tells children that fathers will no longer have any authority in the home.**[78]*
(emphasis added)

Given the decline in church attendance and the amount of single parent families today, I would say that the other side has been pretty successful. The following graph shows the correlation between putting sex education in the schools in 1964 and the rise of single parent families:

---

[77] Quote from the movie, *Agenda: Grinding Down America* by former Idaho State Representative Curtis Bowers
[78] Gloria Lentz, *Raping of Our Children: The Sex Education Scandal*, Arlington House, New Rochelle, N.Y., 1972, p.156

## Single Parent Households
## Female Head, No Spouse Present

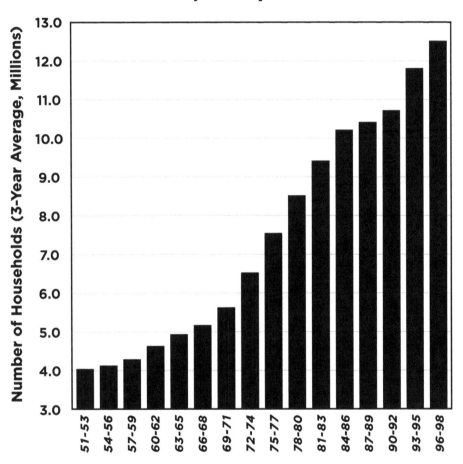

**3-Year Range**
Basic data from Statistical Abstracts of the United States,
and the Department of Commerce, Census Bureau

The more I study those behind the sexual revolution, the more concerned I become! Gabriele Kuby, in her revealing book *The Sexual Revolution: Destruction of Freedom in the Name of Freedom*, summed up why just a few individuals, who are committed to the ideas of humanism, eugenics, and communism, are working so diligently to keep the sexual revolution going:

> *A person rooted in religion and family is hard to manipulate. First the moral bond to belief in God and the social bond to the family must be broken if people are to be seduced by the lure of absolute freedom and free sexual gratification. For decades, increasing prosperity made it possible to sell fun and the meaning of life, with sex front and center. Once the views and behavior of the masses had been altered in this way, the global Cultural Revolution could proceed unhindered through public debate and blatant opposition. Sexualization—even if it's just the occasional fling and a bit of pornography— blinds people and makes them unwilling to resist attacks on the fundamental pillars of society's value system, such as legalization of abortion and homosexual marriage.[79]*

Samuel Adams, a signer of the Declaration of Independence, knew the importance of living chaste and pure lives and the cost to America if this was lost:

> *A general dissolution of principles and manners will more surely overthrow the liberties of America than the whole force of the common enemy.* **While the people are virtuous they cannot be subdued; but when once they lose their virtue they will be ready to surrender the liberties to the first external or internal invader.[80]** (emphasis added)

**Sexual purity is a national security issue!** A person rooted in God's Word can have a successful marriage, healthy children (free of sexual disease and dysfunction), and a closer walk with the Lord (Proverbs 2:1-22). This person has the power of God behind him and cannot be moved (Joshua 23:6-9 and Philippians 4:13).

---

[79] Gabriele Kuby, *The Sexual Revolution: Destruction of Freedom in the Name of Freedom*, Angelico Press, Kettering, OH, 2015, p. 40
[80] William J. Federer, *America's God and Country Encyclopedia of Quotations*, FAME Publishing Inc., U.S.A., 1996, p.23

**I believe that sex education is the foundational pillar that is needed to continue to propel the sexual revolution forward.** How important is sex education to the movements that have come out of the sexual revolution? Let us look at a telling statement made by past president of Planned Parenthood and a signatory of Humanist Manifesto II, the late Alan Guttmacher M.D., when asked a question about how the Supreme Court decision that legalized abortion in January 22, 1973 could be made absolutely secured. He responded with only two words:

*Sex Education.*[81]

The souls of our children are being threatened by the culture of the world today. **What you teach your children or what you allow others to teach your children will either propel the sexual revolution or end it.** In a letter to William Smith during the Revolutionary War, British statesman Edmund Burke stated what happens when we ignore the trends before us:

*All that is necessary for the triumph of evil is that good men do nothing.*[82]

Sex education was once illegal in this country; it was considered "molesting a minor with immoral intent"—up to the age of 21 years—to even mention the words "sexual intercourse" in a classroom.[83] The first state to legalize sex education was Illinois in the 1950s. The Illinois Commission stated why it was important to embrace Kinsey's propaganda that "Children are sexual from birth":

*Children of our times are inadequately trained to live in a free society. The inability of some parents to rear children in a democratic atmosphere and, at the same time, to observe the conventions of society is a fact that needs consideration... [Crime] Prevention through mental hygiene and sex education for both adults and children may prove to be effective. Sex education is more than information about physiological*

---

[81] *Washington Star News*, May 3, 1973
[82] William J. Federer, *America's God and Country-Encyclopedia of Quotations*, Fame Publishing, 1996, p. 82
[83] Richardson O., *Missouri Law Review*, Vol. 38, 1973, p. 397

*functions; it must consider the more subtle emotional attitude toward both sexes and their relationship to one another.*[84]

Planned Parenthood, the pornography industry, and other sex experts were passionate about putting sex education into the classroom. In 1953, Planned Parenthood officials foretold of the **fundamental transformation that was their goal with sex education:**

> *[We must] be ready as educators and parents to **help young people obtain sexual satisfaction before marriage**...and we must be ready to **provide young boys and girls with the best contraception** measures available so they will have the necessary means to achieve sexual satisfaction without having to risk possible pregnancy.*[85] *(emphasis added)*

**If we remain silent, if we ignore and allow the sex education movement to continue, we will lose our children to those who believe our children are "sexual beings."** We could even lose our right to parent our children. The books on family law already reflect the trends that are to come (emphasis added below):

> *Parents can be relied upon to have gender and race biases, so **courts must intervene in a family** on the child's behalf to determine a child's best interest.*

> *Some courts assume that the open homosexuality of a parent is detrimental to the child's interests. This treatment reflects moral judgment, **not a scientific one**, and, even as a moral matter, is subject to considerable societal debate. (Remember it is Kinsey's "science" they are referring to.)*

> ***Marriage, as currently defined in America, has no status,*** *because it "runs counter to the commitment this society avows toward family **diversity**."*[86] *(This was written in 2002, before gay marriage became legal).*

---

[84] The Illinois Commission, 1953, p. 37
[85] Lena Levine, "Psychosocial Development" *Planned Parenthood News*, p. 10 (Summer 1953)
[86] *Principles of the Law of Family Dissolution*, 2002, p.2, 12, 13

Scripture tells us that there is nothing new under the sun, but part of our responsibility as parents is to recognize evil that surrounds our children. God had words of wisdom for us regarding what we are to do with those who promote evil:

> And have no fellowship with the unfruitful works of darkness, but rather expose them. - Ephesians 5:11

I was reminded of how important it is for parents not only to protect their children, but also to expose the evil that is harming them, when I recently attended a "parent preview night" at a local elementary school in my hometown. Although I home school, a few of my friends who had chosen to put their kids in the charter school asked me to tag along and hear what would be presented to their fifth grade boys. By law, sex ed is required in the schools, starting in fifth grade.

The teacher bragged about how the school nurse had searched for a program that would not be *too graphic* but would give them the sexual hygiene information that the children would need. When she passed around the booklets the children would receive, I watched my friends' reactions. They both immediately said, "This is too much!"

What was so telling about the program's results were the statements this teacher made. She first tried to reassure the parents by stating that she had been part of teaching this program to the kids for the last four years. Then I was shocked to hear her admit the following, regarding what the program would do to the children:

> It will take the kids a few days to get over the shock of it [the information].

> They [the kids] will be 'shell-shocked' and it will be the quietest day at carpool all year.

> They will feel like they have lost their childhood.

Wow! This teacher was so indoctrinated by her sex education training that **she saw nothing wrong with shocking or taking away children's innocence!** Sex education is meant to train children to look at themselves as sexual beings, and given the earlier statements by Dr. Miriam Grossman, this information *does* cause stress to children and it *does* put them in shock. Remember—sexual words and images are powerful!

My heart went out to my two friends; they were the only parents in the room to openly object to the content. Another parent tried to convince my friends to put their kids into the program despite how they felt; she reasoned that their children would probably hear the information from other kids anyway. The same parent stressed that my friends would much rather their children get the information from the "trained sex educator" first. As one of my friends was leaving the room, she overheard the other moms calling both of them "frantic parents."

This is what we are up against. **Sex education is so widely accepted, and now mandatory in the schools, that we no longer question it as parents.** To object would mean to go against the flow or be in the minority.

What would you do if you were in their situation? I can tell you that both moms pulled their sons out of the school not only for the *hygiene class*, but also for the day. One of these moms emailed me later to tell me the reasons why she took her son out—and she also made her reasons known to the school officials. She gave me permission to share her reasons with you:

1.  The material covers sexual reproduction outside the context of morals and modesty.

2.  The material is a one-size-fits-all approach presented to *young children* at different levels of maturity.

3.  Imparting values and responsibility is my job as a parent, not the State of Texas or the education system. (I don't expect public schools to even hint at God's plan for marriage!).

4.  My child is a precious gift, entrusted to me by God, that I am responsible for shepherding. I won't put him in the hands of a stranger to share information on sexual reproduction. The school can teach him his ABCs and 123s, but not this.

Now in the twenty-first century, our children are receiving lessons in schools regarding morals, but those morals aren't coming from the Bible. Instead, our children are being taught moral relativism, which states, "Whatever I deem to be morally right in my own eyes is what I should do." I would go so far as to say, some of these programs and some of these educators are preparing the children for sexual abuse. Due to the legalization of pornography and sex education, sexual abuse and the sex trafficking of children are rapidly rising.

A school nurse in Chicago sent me a book that has a picture of a boy hugging an adult man on the cover, and the title of the book is *Unequal Partners*. This was a program written by Planned Parenthood and is meant to be an aid to school officials to help children if they are in a sexual relationship with an adult. Unfortunately, the help offered is not to call the police but something very different:

> *Unequal Partners helps teachers, counselors, nurses, and other professionals **educate young people (ten to seventeen years old) to make healthy decisions about relationships**, especially those involving the power imbalances that can occur when there are significant age differences.*[87] (emphasis mine)

According to this book, a ten-year-old boy having sex with an adult male may not be unhealthy. It is no longer socially *un*acceptable for adults to entice and rape children. Sex education is openly taking a much darker turn!

God's Word teaches us the opposite of what is being taught by the field of human sexuality, the opposite of what is being taught in sex education classes across the country. God not only gives us clear moral guidelines to follow to keep us healthy, He also reminds us of who we are in Him:

> *Do you not know that the unrighteous will not inherit the kingdom of God? Do not be deceived. Neither fornicators, nor idolaters, nor adulterers, nor homosexuals ("effeminate" in the KJV), nor sodomites ("abusers of themselves with mankind" in the KJV), nor thieves, nor covetous, nor drunkards, nor revilers, nor extortioners will inherit the kingdom of God. And such were some of you. But you were washed, but you were*

---

[87] Sue Montfort and Peggy Brick, *Unequal Partners: Teaching about Power and Consent in Adult-Teen and Other Relationships*, Planned Parenthood of Greater Northern New Jersey, Inc., Morristown, NJ, 2007

*sanctified in the name of the Lord Jesus and by the Spirit of our God. - I Corinthians 6: 9-10*

While writing this book, I am also helping with my oldest son's upcoming wedding. This is the son, who nineteen years ago, was entering Kindergarten when I was beginning this battle against sex education in the Lutheran Church. He is in the military now, and he has always stayed committed to remain pure until marriage. Despite being teased by some of his fellow shipmen for being the lone virgin on his vessel, others have admired his self-control.

In addition to teaching our children about chastity, purity, modesty, and self-control, my husband and I have always taught our children that God has chosen the person whom they will marry. In God's timing He would bring them together, but until that time, they were to focus on what God wanted them to do on this earth and live their single lives in purity for Him. They were to be patient and wait on God's timing.

When my son took an assignment to a remote island, I never dreamed he could possibly meet his future soul mate during that time. However, I have been proven wrong—and I was reminded that God can bring two people together in the most secluded of places on His planet! It has been a pure joy to watch my son group-date and then court this lovely young Christian woman. He proposed over Thanksgiving, and now the wedding plans are in full swing. Two young people who were committed to purity will begin a new relationship with no baggage, no guilt. Praise the Lord!

I have been very honored and blessed to speak to parent groups all over the country. Often, after hearing of the plan behind the attack on our children and our nation, parents will ask me, "What can I do to fight this?" My answer every time is: **Raise up your children in the fear and admonishment of the Lord. Teach your children about purity and how they can honor God, their families, and themselves with their words and actions.**

My friend Heather McEwan has spent years informing parents in her native country of Australia of the origins of sex education. She ended one of her presentations by beautifully encapsulating the vision we should all have for our youth:

*I have a vision of a group of youth: girls who know their value and keep their virtue for whom it is intended; boys who, through courage and godly revelation of manhood, can withstand the cultural tide and retain their virtue, also; young people who are immersed in the job of growing up—to learn to find their place in the world and to seek out God's plan for their lives rather than be preoccupied by a progression of temporary romantic entanglements.*

Well said Heather! **Let's start a trend with our children. Let's deal with our past, raise a generation of children who strive for purity, and hence, change the course of our nation and the world!**

**REMEMBER: THE SEXUAL REVOLUTION CAN CONTINUE WITH OUR CHILDREN OR IT CAN END WITH OUR CHILDREN!**

*And do not be conformed to this world, but be transformed by the renewing of your mind, that you may prove what is that good and acceptable and perfect will of God. - Romans 12:2*

*Do not be overcome with evil, but overcome evil with good. - Romans 12:21*

**Suggested Resources**

*RSVP America Training Manual*, www.rsvpamerica.org

René Wormser, *FOUNDATIONS: Their Power and Influence*

Judith Reisman, *Kinsey, Crimes, & Consequences* and *Sexual Sabotage: How One Mad Scientist Unleashed a Plague of Corruption and Contagion on America*

Gabriele Kuby, *The Global Sexual Revolution:Destruction of Freedom in the Name of Freedom*

Dr. Miriam Grossman, *You're Teaching my Child What?*

Karen Booth, *Forgetting How to Blush:United Methodism's Compromise with the Sexual Revolution*

Dr. Meg Meeker, *Epidemic: How Teen Sex is Killing our Kids*

Francis A. Schaeffer, *The Christian Manifesto*

First Principles Press, *Endowed by Their Creator: A Collection of Historic Military Prayers 1774-Present*

Mark Batterson, *The Circle Maker* and *Draw the Circle*

Stormie Omartian, *The Power of a Praying Wife* and *The Power of a Praying Parent*

Dutch Sheets, *Praying for America*

Tony Evans, *The Battle is the Lord's*

Erwin W. Lutzer, *Who are You to Judge? Learning to Distinguish between Truths, Half-truths and Lies*

Voddie T. Baucham Jr., *Family Driven Faith-Doing What it Takes to Raise Sons and Daughters who Walk with God*

D. James Kennedy, *What if America were a Christian Nation Again?*

Ed Bulkley, Ph.D., *Why Christians Can't Trust Psychology*

Ray C. Stedman, *Spiritual Warfare: How to Stand Firm in the Faith*

Kay Arthur, *Lord, Is It Warfare? Teach Me to Stand*

John Eckhardt, *Prayers that Rout Demons: Prayers for Defeating Demons and Overthrowing the Power of Darkness*

Derek Prince, *They Shall Expel Demons: What You Need to Know about Demons, Your Invisible Enemies*

Frank Damazio, *Seasons of Intercession: God's Call to Prayer-Intercessors for Every Believer*

Cindy Jacobs, *Possessing the Gates of the Enemy: A Training Manual for Militant Intercession*

Dennis Rainey, *A Call to Family Reformation: Restoring the Soul of America One Home at a Time*

# Concluding Thoughts

Thank you for taking the time to read this book. We were all born in the middle of the sexual revolution, so this material can be challenging. We were raised to be much less modest than our forefathers ever were. I also realize this information can be shocking and could anger you, as it did me. After I attended my first RSVP America training and learned who was behind the sexual revolution, their intent, and how evil their foundation really is, I couldn't sleep that night.

Most parents don't know where sex education came from or its intention for us and our children. Growing up believing that we were sexual beings and having it pounded into us did us great harm.

I so badly wanted sex education to be the answer that would solve the problem of sexually active teens. I wanted to believe that what I had been told was true—that talking to kids about sex would decrease the pregnancy and venereal disease rates. I had hoped that sex education would be a path with a healthy outcome. Why? There were really two main reasons.

The first reason is because I had been teaching it myself for five years as a school nurse, and I wanted to know that I had helped, and not contributed to the problems kids, teens, and adults face. I wanted to believe that those who had encouraged me to talk openly and graphically about sex had not misled me;

The second reason I wanted sex education to be correct was because my church, my denomination, and the entire body of Christ also promoted it. I *did not* want the church to be in error. I *did not* want to be the person who would have to approach those in the church with this error.

However, as I researched sex education, I found that it was not *helpful*—it was *harmful* for children. Every layer I pulled away led right back to the same evil foundation. One author, who was listed as a resource for the *Learning About Sex* series, once worked with the "Lucifer Trust."[88] **How much more obvious can this evil be?**

A pastor in our area once preached five sermons on sexuality and shared about a favorite book he used as a resource. That book's bibliography lists two authors who not only were Kinsey's associates, they promoted pedophilia as normal and healthy. Another author of a famous Christian women's book on sexuality listed a former director of the Kinsey Institute in her bibliography! So many in the church are using Kinsey's fraudulent science, and they don't even know it.

As a result of circumstances and facts I was learning, I believe God impressed me to speak out, and a ministry now called **The Matthew XVIII Group** was birthed. The scripture which provides the foundation for the ministry is Matthew 18:15-17:

> *Moreover, if your brother sins against you, go and tell him his fault between you and him alone. If he hears you, you have gained a brother. But if he will not hear, take with you one or two more, that by the mouth of two or three witnesses every word may be established. And if he refuses to hear them, tell it to the church.*

If my husband and I didn't believe this was God's calling for us, we would not have survived some of the heartbreaking moments that have occurred since then. My husband was forced out of ministerial work, due to our position on sexual purity, and we continue to witness Christian leaders boldly using Kinsey's "science" in their sexuality messages.

What has helped us weather the storms are the incredible moments God has provided, demonstrating His power and direction. One such example: the former Inspector General for the Department of Defense and a Louisiana Supreme Court Justice, both godly men,

---

[88] *Understanding Sex* by Lester Kirkendall is listed in the bibliography of the original *Learning About Sex* series of 1968. He was not only the former president of the American Humanist Association, once on the board for Planned Parenthood, and past director of SIECUS—but was also assisting in the operations of an organization called the "Temple of Understanding," which uses funds donated by the tax-free Lucis Trust organization, the organization that published the "Lucifer" magazine. See Claire Chambers, *The SIECUS Circle: A Humanist Revolution*, Western Islands Belmont, MA, 1977, pp.30-36

thanked me for this ministry and what is being accomplished. Also, Colonel Ron Ray—former Assistant to the Secretary of Defense during the Reagan administration, retired Marine, constitutional lawyer, and American patriot—not only helped me make the case to the Lutheran Concordia Publishing Company about why the *Learning About Sex* series was in error, but he told me that he "had my back." Only God can orchestrate that!

"Who am *I*? I'm just a mom," was my common refrain spoken to Eunice Ray of RSVP America. She would always encourage me and then introduce me to amazing people, such as the ones listed above. Yes, God can use "just a mom," and He most often takes the simple of this world to confound the wise; All He is looking for is one who will say "Here am I." I have learned that when God calls you to a task, He will equip you for that task, often in amazing ways.

My prayer and hope for this book is to accomplish two things:

First, to expose the darkness in the use of Kinsey's fraudulent science in Christian sex education materials. In doing so, you as a parent can make an educated decision about how you want to approach the subject matter. Hopefully the information provided within these pages answered the question about why you felt uncomfortable about having the "sex talk" with your child, and provided peace for your decision process.

Second, to encourage and inspire parents to return to how we once taught children about the *facts of life* and how it was accomplished by talking about God's life process in a modest, biblical way. Doing things God's way—using His Word as our guide—has given my husband and me peace and confidence in our parenting skills.

The Word of God is clear about what is sexually moral and what is not.

Our laws once reflected God's Word; however, now that those laws have been removed, man-made laws legalize every immoral sex act. All appears hopeless. But we as the body of Christ can do something about that—and it begins with our children! There *is* hope and God can turn any situation around no matter how hopeless it may seem.

Here are steps you can take:

1.  Model purity for your children in all you say and do.

2.  Approach the topic with modesty.

3.  Remind your children of their identity in Christ.

4.  Don't use the word "sex."

5.  Teach self-control.

6.  Use God's words, found in scriptures, when having a conversation about the facts of life.

7.  When your child asks a question, ask him or her more questions first before answering.

8.  Look at your children through Jesus' eyes and not the human sexuality experts' eyes.

9.  Maintain your child's moral innocence, without keeping them naïve.

10. Through prayer, along with the help of God and His instruction found in scripture, you and your children can help end the evil coming out of the sexual revolution.

There are parents standing up to sex education in their children's schools, and it is gaining momentum. Here are just a few headlines of those who are making a difference:

**Omaha, NE:** "Parents strike back on sex ed...and win."[89]

**Massachusetts:** "Mother makes shocking video to counter lies by school about x-rated pornography."[90]

**Missouri:** "Parents group fighting aggressive LGBT sex-ed curriculum being forced by School Board in suburban St. Louis"[91]

---

[89] https://www.onenewsnow.com/education/2016/12/16/parents-strike-back-on-sex-ed-and-win
[90] http://www.massresistance.org/index.html
[91] http://www.massresistance.org/docs/gen3/16c/MO-MassResistance_sex-ed/index.html

**At the national and international level:** "Comprehensive Sexuality Education (CSE) goes far beyond sex ed, and is a dangerous assault on the health and innocence of children..."[92]

**In Croatia:** "Stunner! Court kills Kinsey sex ed nationally."[93]

There are efforts all over the world to combat sex education! **We have trusted the "sex education experts" for too long. It is time to redeem this teaching, and with God's help, I believe America can follow Croatia's lead!**

Should your children already be involved in fornication, pornography, sodomy, etc., there is still hope. Yes, it will require lots of prayer and lots of love. Because so many children and adults now see their primary identity as a false "sexual identity," entire communities have arisen, held together by a particular sexual identity. From LGBTQ to SMBD, these people need our compassion and help.

Because of broken homes, because of child sex abuse, because we have stopped teaching our children about what it means to be men and women, there is much confusion in our world. The fact that our nation has removed God's Law as the foundation for our moral standard and replaced it with new laws based on Kinsey has not helped. As we learn how to navigate this brave new world, let us remember that we are to always demonstrate God's love to the sinner while not condoning the sin. **Please love your children unconditionally, but don't ignore God's truth in the process.**

**So, what am I asking you to do? To make a paradigm shift; actually, to make a *"Purity Paradigm Shift."*** Prayerfully consider all of the information you have just read. Spend more time getting to know the God of Scripture, and then be sure to diligently teach the scriptures to your kids. Teaching children and youth about pregnancy and venereal disease has not worked. *I believe the answer to the onslaught of the sexual agenda today is to raise up a generation of children who have a firm foundation in Christ Jesus.* He is the One who will define their thoughts, actions, and decisions for the future.

---

[92] http://www.comprehensivesexualityeducation.org/
[93] http://www.wnd.com/2013/05/stunner-courtkills-kinsey-sexed-nationally/

*And let us not grow weary while doing good, for in due season we shall reap if we do not lose heart. Therefore, as we have opportunity, let us do good to all, especially to those who are of the household of faith. - Galatians 6:9-10*

I will close with this beautiful prayer from *The Soldier's Prayer Book of 1861:*

*O MOST powerful and glorious Lord God, the Lord of Hosts, that rulest and commandest all things; thou sittest in the throne judging right; And therefore we make our address to thy Divine Majesty, in this our necessity, that thou wouldest take the cause into thine own hand, and judge between us and our enemies. Stir up thy strength, O Lord, and come and help us; for thou givest not always the battle to the strong, but canst save by many or by few. O let not our sins now cry against us for vengeance; but hear us they poor servants begging mercy, and imploring thy help, and that thou wouldest be a defense unto us against the face of the enemy. Make it appear that thou art our Savior and mighty Deliverer, through Jesus Christ our Lord. Amen.[94]*

## For More Information on this subject:

1. Consider taking the following online courses from Master's International University of Divinity:  "Restoring Biblical Purity in the Church" (RBP 1500) and "An Investigation of Sex Education, Abstinence, and Purity: Saving the Next Generation from Sexual Disease and Dysfunction" (SAP 1500). These classes can be audited or taken for college credit and are offered in the months of January, September, and November, with a live on-site three day seminar in May (where RBP & SAP are taught, as well as "Spiritual Warfare").  Participants are parents, grandparents, and faith leaders from all over the world.  For more information go to:

   http://ims.mdivs.edu/students-alumni/online-seminars/

---

[94] *Endowed by Their Creator: A Collection of Historic American Military Prayers: 1774-present,* p. 44

2. The Matthew XVIII Group ministry also provides information regarding the sex education battle inside and outside of the church. Please go to our website, www.matthewxviii.org or Facebook page at https://www.facebook.com/MatthewXVIII/

3. To combat sex education in your district, go to the STOP CSE Coalition which comprises a network of individuals fighting sex education at state level in the U.S. and also at the U.N. level:

   http://www.comprehensivesexualityeducation.org/

Again, thank you for your time. It has been an honor to write this book for you, and please look forward to more books on biblical purity soon!

# About Audrey Werner

Audrey Werner is founder and president of THE MATTHEW XVIII GROUP whose goal is to restore purity to homes, churches, and the nation through education via public speaking engagements, online, and printed materials. This ministry uses the Matthew 18:15-17 process to approach Christian leaders who are using Kinsey's fraudulent and criminal "science," with the hope that once error is identified, Kinsey's works can be purged from Christian resources.

As a former public and private school sex education teacher and STD/HIV nurse, Audrey Werner saw first-hand the dangerous outcomes of teaching sex ed to children. Because of her background with sex ed and her extensive research, she is now known as the "Sex Education Expert" about Christian sex education programs for the Advisory Board of the American Academy of Biblical Counselors and for the Expose Comprehensive Sex Education (CSE) Coalition.

She was certified by the Michigan Department of Public Health in HIV counseling and testing and by the CDC for STD counseling, testing, and treatment. Her clinical experience also included pregnancy testing and counseling of teens, as well as distribution of birth control to minors without parental consent.

Audrey is a national speaker for RSVP America, which is a campaign that was designed to respond to America's spiraling societal decline in the second half of the 20th century. The mission of RSVP America is to restore social virtue and purity to America by educating and equipping grassroots activists to effect law, legislation, and public policy at all levels of government. (The Matthew XVIII Group ministry is an offshoot of RSVP and serves to work directly with the Christian Church).

Audrey has worked with leaders from *Concerned Women for America, Missouri* and *Texas Eagle Forum* on matters related to the root of sex education.

Currently, she serves as Dean of Life Issues and Professor at Master's International University of Divinity, where she teaches courses on sex education and the sexual revolution. Her students include pastors and other faith leaders from all over the world.

Audrey has been married for 31 years to her husband Joe who served as the Director of Christian Education in the Lutheran Church Missouri Synod. Together they have four children and one daughter-in-law.

.

Printed in the USA
CPSIA information can be obtained
at www.ICGtesting.com
LVHW021505151023
761145LV00013B/966